HOME DESIGN WORKBOOKS

BATHROOM

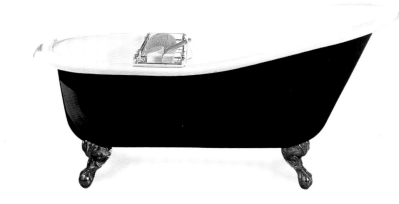

HOME DESIGN WORKBOOKS
BATHROOM

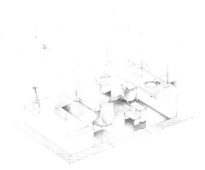

SUZANNE ARDLEY

DORLING KINDERSLEY

LONDON • NEW YORK • SYDNEY • MOSCOW

A DORLING KINDERSLEY BOOK

Project Editor BELLA PRINGLE
Project Art Editor SHARON MOORE
DTP Designer MARK BRACEY
Photographer JAKE FITZJONES
Stylist FIONA CRAIG-MCFEELY
Production Controller ALISON JONES
Series Editor CHARLOTTE DAVIES
Series Art Editor CLIVE HAYBALL

First published in Great Britain in 1998 by
Dorling Kindersley Limited
9 Henrietta Street, London WC2E 8PS

Copyright © 1998 Dorling Kindersley Limited, London
Text copyright © 1998 Suzanne Ardley

Visit us on the World Wide Web at
http://www.dk.com

A CIP catalogue record for this book
is available from the British Library

ISBN 0 7513 03771

Text film output in Great Britain by R & B Creative Services Ltd
Reproduced in Singapore by Pica
Printed by Neografia, Slovakia

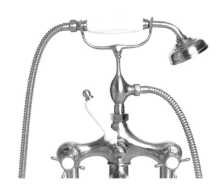

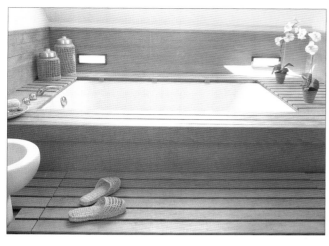

ROOM PLANS • 46

PLAN YOUR DESIGN • 76

CONTENTS

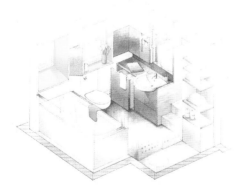

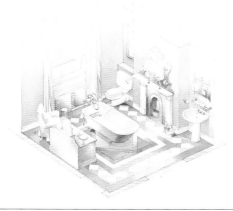

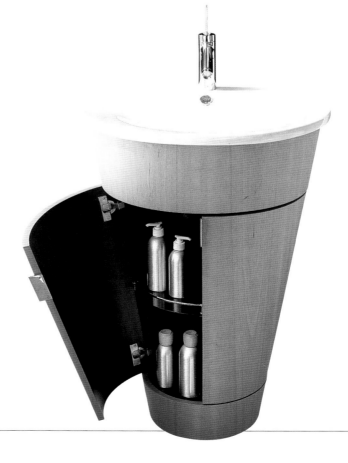

INTRODUCTION

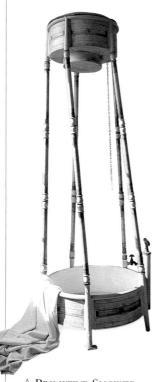

△ **PRIMITIVE SHOWER**
Taking a shower rather than a bath was considered eccentric when this portable shower was made in the 1800s. The innovative design has a tank supported by mock-bamboo poles and, on pulling the lever, water is released through the fixed shower head, and collects in the foot bowl.

THE BATHROOM is probably the most personal and private room in the house and one which is in frequent use. The success of a bathroom design relies on taking into account the demands that will be made on the room. Will it be a functional bathroom for a busy family or a luxurious room, purely for one's own use, in which to relax. Bathrooms are no longer regarded simply as utilitarian washrooms where cleansing rituals are performed out of sight behind closed doors. They are congenial spaces where you can surround yourself with well-designed, practical, and aesthetic objects that reflect both your lifestyle and taste.

More than ever, people expect bathrooms to fulfil a range of functions, and are happy to re-fit the existing bathroom, convert a spare room into a bathroom, or add a bathroom ensuite so that they can indulge in everything from a bracing wake-up shower or soothing hot spa, to the exclusivity of a bathroom-cum-dressing-room. Even where space is tight, clever planning and positioning of sanitaryware can ensure time spent in the bathroom is truly pleasurable.

BATHROOM INFLUENCES

My initial interest in bathroom design was awakened by a visit to Fiji some years ago when visiting old family friends in the Nausoris. Their remote Colonial-style house had a wonderfully simple but effective shower system. Fed by a rainwater tank hidden in the treetops, ice-cold water coursed through a hosepipe to a colossal shower head towering above the cubicle. No half-way measures here: plunging into the deluge, you

▽ BATHING IN GRANDEUR
Kingston Lacy was one of the first stately
homes in England to install a bathroom
on a grand scale. Before plumbing was
fitted in the 1920s, servants filled the
bath and washstand with hot water.

◁ BOLD AND SIMPLE
Simple lines and uncluttered
surfaces are the mainstay of
modern bathroom design.
Durable, low-maintenance
materials cater for busy
people with limited time
for keeping the bathroom
spotlessly clean.

were left gasping and drenched in cold water
from head to toe. Having experienced my first
invigorating "power shower", I was convinced
that showers were as therapeutic as they were
cleansing and, on my return to England, tried
to recreate the same showering experience.

EARLY WASHING FACILITIES

In stark contrast to the old saying "cleanliness
is next to Godliness", early domestic washing
facilities were as basic, but less effective, than my
shower in Fiji, and consisted of a bowl and a
pitcher of water placed in a corner of the bedroom.
There were no bathrooms but, on occasion, a
portable bath tub was brought into the room
and filled by hand with water heated on the fire.
Family members would take it in turns to bathe
in the same water. It was impractical to take a
bath on a daily basis so odours were masked with
scents, such as lavender, bergamot, and rosemary.

1930s BATHROOM ▷
1930s BATHROOM ▷
Demand for bathroom facilities grew in the 1930s which led to a wider choice of sanitaryware including this type of pedestal basin; coloured suites rather than white suites were considered to be luxury items.

△ **RETRO LOOK**
Modern technology joins forces here with classic 1930s style to give a heated towel rail that looks good and works efficiently.

By the mid-1800s, purpose-built bathrooms began to be installed, but only in grander houses. These bathrooms were furnished comfortably like other rooms in the house, but instead of displaying elegant bureaus and dining tables, they had ornate washstands, dressing tables, and baths. These early bathrooms helped the rich distinguish themselves from the "great unwashed", at a time when people began to understand that dirt carried germs and potentially fatal diseases.

FORM AND STYLE

In time, soft furnishings and ornate details were considered inappropriate for bathrooms as they gather dirt and dust, and so the room evolved a colder, more clinical appearance. Plain white tubs, tiling, and metal fixtures became the norm.

By the 1940s, pressed steel baths with hand-held showers were being mass-produced, enabling more homes to own a bath, but apart from some patterned porcelain and plain-coloured suites, bathrooms remained functional and hidden away.

BATHROOM COLOURS

The 1970s and 1980s saw a growth in the range of coloured suites and unusual bath shapes fuelled by a desire for exclusivity, while near the turn of this century, the minimalist metal, glass, and mosaic designs reign supreme. Despite the hi-tech movement, traditional sanitaryware and fittings have undergone a revival with roll-top baths, classic brass shower roses, deep mahogany panelling, and ornate furnishings becoming increasingly popular. Modern reproductions abound, but for lovers of authenticity, original sanitaryware is available, restored to its former glory by specialist retailers. Taps and fittings, ball-jointed radiators, and wrought-iron clothes horses complete this nostalgic dip into the past, recreating its own distinct and decadent style.

ADDITIONAL FACILITIES

Today, a comfortable bathroom is taken for granted, and now in family homes we have come to expect a second bathroom or a separate shower room to prevent a bottleneck of users at peak times. House builders appreciate this trend and second bathrooms, particularly an ensuite bathroom or shower room leading off the master bedroom, are fast becoming a standard specification in new-build homes. Property developers and estate agents agree that an extra bathroom increases both the desirability and value of your home.

The popularity of the second bathroom has also been fuelled by the development of space-saving sanitaryware designs and ventilation systems. It is now possible to fit ensuite facilities into the smallest of spaces – a feat that would have been impossible in the past.

INNOVATIVE DESIGN

Bathroom design has now become a state-of-the-art industry, combining form and function with the latest technology. In addition to a huge choice of baths and showers, and bath/shower modules, a spectacular range of sanitaryware

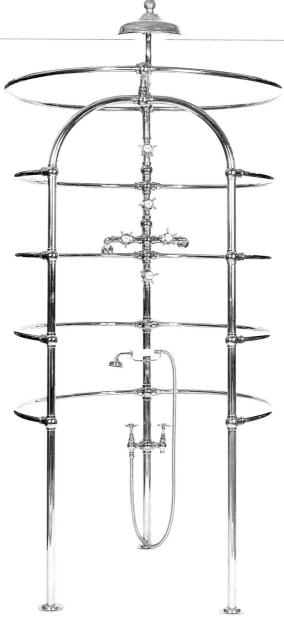

◁ **NEEDLE SHOWER 1910** Early enthusiasts of showers would have been impressed by this striking design with its overhead shower rose and a series of body sprays from the circular tubes that created the first all-round shower.

▽ **JACUZZI SHOWER** Showers over baths are not new, but Jacuzzi's all-in-one system is designed to fit into the space of a standard bath. The power shower capsule and sleek bath shape make bathing highly enjoyable.

products offer hydrotherapy, steam cleansing, lymph stimulation, and body toning systems. The introduction to the industry of ceramic disc technology now enables a single-lever mixer (with just one handle and spout) to deliver an even temperature and flow of water. The ceramic disc creates an ultra-smooth action as you turn the tap on and off, the mixer does not drip, and it resists limescale build-up in hardwater areas. Booster pumps have also had their part to play by improving water pressure and overall shower performance. Water temperatures can now

▽ CONTEMPORARY TAP
Ceramic disc technology has led to single lever taps that control both the flow rate and temperature mix of the water smoothly and effortlessly.

be pre-set for adults and children, while as an additional safety measure, unbearably hot water from the shower head will cut out instantly to prevent scalding. These small but highly significant developments in bathroom technology have transformed the face of the ordinary bathroom, making it more efficient, safe, and fun to use.

ENVIRONMENTAL CONCERNS

In response to the arrival of new bathroom materials, finishes, and fittings, manufacturers have developed a host of cleaning chemicals to keep your bathroom in pristine condition. There are products that prevent and remove limescale deposits, chemicals that dissolve residue left by soaps and oils, and substances to irradicate stubborn mildew. But the use of these harsh chemicals combined with the dramatic increase in the amount of water required by each household to sustain more than one bathroom, is creating serious environmental problems. Responsible manufacturers are addressing these issues by developing products, especially wc cisterns, that use less water to flush than models currently in production. At present, 7.5 litres (1.6 gallons) of water are needed to flush the wc but with design improvements being researched by manufacturers, this is likely to be reduced.

Much can be done by individuals to save water when using the bathroom on a daily basis. Remember, a shower uses up much less water than running a full bath so, if possible, try to take more showers. Another small but important step is to remember to turn off the tap rather

△ MODERN MATERIALS
This well-considered wc design with a hidden cistern combines durable stainless steel with the beauty of a clear acrylic seat which is warm to the touch.

than leaving it running while cleaning your teeth. Also ensure that taps do not drip, a huge amount of water can be wasted this way.

PLANNING YOUR BATHROOM

Many bathrooms are as intensively planned and as expensive to install as kitchens; the plumbing and drainage pipes, electrical points, and heating and ventilation systems all need to be accurately placed within the room, and must comply with health and safety regulations.

When designing the space, aim to arrive at a solution that suits your lifestyle. Consider what demands will be made on the bathroom, how much time will be spent in it, and who will use it. The time you devote to this and assessing the advantages and disadvantages of bathroom hardware will be rewarded when you emerge from a room that leaves you feeling a hundred times better than when you went in.

WHAT DO YOU WANT FROM YOUR BATHROOM?

Before purchasing a range of expensive sanitaryware and fittings, analyse your lifestyle and bathing habits, and decide which family members are going to use the new bathroom. To help you arrive at a solution, compare the benefits of the bathroom facilities below.

❶ A space that can be shared with others.

❷ A bathroom equipped with child safety features.

❸ A room that doubles up as a dressing room.

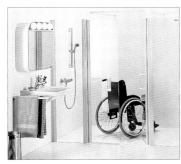

❹ Facilities that less-abled people can easily use.

❺ A comfortably furnished bathroom in which to relax.

❻ A fitted bathroom where everything can be put away.

❼ A bathroom that makes the best use of a small area.

❽ A shower room rather than a bathroom.

❾ Maximum comfort from existing facilities.

HOW CAN THIS SPACE WORK FOR YOU?

Whatever the shape or size of your existing bathroom you will want to get the most from the products you choose. Decide how suitable the room is for the items you wish to include and what alterations, if any, will be required.

☐ Is your present bathroom big enough for you and your family's needs or would converting a spare bedroom into a large bathroom be a better planning solution?

☐ Would choosing compact sanitaryware designs enable you to squeeze a shower, bath, and other items of sanitaryware into a limited space, or would a separate shower room be a better solution?

☐ Is the bathroom lighting good enough to see when shaving or applying cosmetics, or could it be improved by a second window or specialist lighting around the mirror or basin area?

CHOOSING A STYLE ▷
This fresh white bathroom combines a range of style details that are subtlely co-ordinated. Little touches, such as an ethnic terracotta pot holding lavatory paper, family photos, and fresh flowers present an elegant but well-furnished look.

△ **FORM AND FUNCTION**
High-quality fittings will enhance both the look and the performance of an otherwise ordinary item of sanitaryware. Choose an attractive design with a simple, smooth operation.

The style choices you make for your bathroom are personal and need to be carefully thought through. Your selection of products is crucial. Fixtures and fittings must last well, and still look good after several years' wear and tear. To help you decide what elements you wish to include in your brand-new or re-modelled bathroom, establish what you like and dislike about the existing room. Ask yourself questions, such as: How easy is it to step in and out of the bath? How warm is the bathroom on cold winter mornings? Is the sanitaryware easy to clean? Is the shower powerful enough? Also, consider the

architectural features in the room itself, such as decorative plasterwork and the windows, and how they will affect the finished look. Before pulling everything out and starting from scratch, stop to ask whether some of the existing elements might fit equally well with the style of your new bathroom plan.

STYLE PREFERENCES

As regards my own personal style, as much as I love the simplicity of contemporary bathroom design and innovative new materials, I feel most comfortable in rooms that have an informal,

◁ CHOOSING THE ELEMENTS
Look for attractive designs that also help with
your storage. This modern pedestal basin has a
compartment for storing towels and a ledge on
which to rest soaps when washing your hands.

of reach of young children and, if you choose
a back-to-wall wc, the cistern will be boxed in
behind a half-height false wall, or tongue and
groove panelling creating a display shelf on top
for attractive bottles and jars.

CHARACTER AND FUNCTION

Once you have decided what style you favour,
look for sanitaryware, materials, and fittings that
will add the desired character but are, above all,
functional. Collect manufacturers' brochures
outlining the specification of each product
to help you make informed decisions. In the
chapter featuring *Bathroom Elements*, both
the advantages and disadvantages of the major
bathroom products are outlined. For example,
if you have young children you will be able to
judge whether ceramic tiles or rubber flooring is
best. Whatever element you are considering, take

lived-in atmosphere. Objects that are displayed
because you like them or simply because they
have been handed down to you, achieve a warm
personal look that others, selected merely to
present an image, often lack. In the same way,
a clever blend of contemporary and traditional
pieces can produce spectacular results, so even
if your bathroom is in an old house, do not feel
limited to furnishing it with period pieces.

Whatever your style preferences, try to plan
as much storage space as possible in your new
bathroom so that items do not clutter up
countertops and other activity areas. Place only
attractive objects on display, and keep utilitarian
items hidden behind closed doors. Toiletries,
lavatory paper, cleaning materials, medicines,
and first aid boxes take up a considerable space.
Installing a semi-countertop basin, with storage
units beneath is one solution. Shelves around the
walls at shoulder-height can be used to display
decorative accessories, while keeping them out

WHAT COULD YOU CHANGE?

Use the following
checklist to help you
pinpoint what it is
about your bathroom
that you would like
to improve or replace.
□ Change shape of
existing room.
□ Alter architectural
features.
□ Improve access to
natural light.
□ Upgrade sanitaryware
and fittings.
□ Renew tiling and
waterproof seals.
□ Replace flooring.
□ Redesign lighting.
□ Add shaving sockets.
□ Improve ventilation
and heating.
□ Reorganize plumbing.
□ Reduce noise levels.
□ Increase privacy.
□ Reorganize available
storage space.
□ Rethink the size,
height, and position
of sanitaryware.
□ Change furniture.
□ Update all curtains,
blinds and other soft
furnishings.

◁ CHOOSING DETAILS
Most bathroom bottles,
pots, containers, and tubes
are small. Plan separate shelf
compartments so items can
be stored and found easily.
Mirror-fronted cabinets
also reflect light. Choose a
lockable design to protect
children from danger.

PLAN OF ACTION

Having decided on the style and elements you wish to include, use this checklist before starting alterations to ensure that nothing has been overlooked.

☐ Have you received permission from the relevant authorities for additional plumbing fixtures, or planning consent for structural alterations?

☐ Will you need the help of professionals or will you be able to do most of the work yourself?

☐ Are you planning to renovate or re-enamel items of sanitaryware, for example, a cast iron bath? Do you need help having it taken out?

☐ Have you costed the total job and received quotes for the work you cannot do yourself?

☐ Have you allowed a little extra money in the budget for finishing decoration and soft furnishings?

into account its practicality in a bathroom environment as daily contact with heat, steam, and splashes of water soon cause inferior materials to deteriorate.

It is not just the sanitaryware that needs to be attractive and functional in bathrooms but also the lighting, wallcoverings, window treatments, furniture, and cabinet surfaces. Good lighting makes a bathroom safer to use, well-chosen flooring will be both hardwearing and comfortable underfoot, and the right cabinet finish can transform the look of the bathroom and offer a water-resistant surface. These considerations present an opportunity to influence the look of the room while achieving a comfortable bathroom that is simple to maintain.

IDEAS INTO REALITY

This book is intended to help you to arrive at an ergonomic design with items arranged for ease of use and visual pleasure.

If your bathroom plans are ambitious – for example, if the room needs to be extended to accommodate the sanitaryware or you are adding a second bathroom in the attic – you should also consult a qualified architect. An architect will want to look at your proposed bathroom before start of work so that he or she can advise you on building regulations, and he will also organize every detail of the job from beginning to end, and inspect on-going work to check it is of a satisfactory standard and on schedule. Architects will also be able to recommend a good team of plumbers, fitters, and electricians. If you want to create a bathroom that satisfies all your needs, however, your input is vital, so use the following pages to help you formulate your design ideas before putting them into practice.

HOW THIS BOOK WORKS

THIS BOOK gives you the practical know-how you need to design a bathroom that matches your lifestyle, and to create an efficient and comfortable space. It will help you plan a new bathroom or adapt an existing one. A series of questions helps you assess what you need from your bathroom, then a survey of fixtures and fittings helps you to choose the right elements for your room. Next, three-dimensional plans of seven bathrooms explain how to engineer a successful design, and finally, there are instructions on drawing up a bathroom plan.

2. SELECT FITTINGS ▽

To help you compile a list of the features that will best suit your requirements, a range of sanitaryware, fixtures, and furniture are surveyed (*pp. 20– 45*). A "remember" box draws your attention to important design points, and the advantages and disadvantages of each element are discussed. Simple diagrams demonstrate how to use and where to position your sanitaryware and furniture for maximum safety, comfort, and efficiency.

1. IDENTIFY YOUR NEEDS ▽

A number of preliminary questions (*pp. 18–19*) are asked to encourage you to think about your bathroom needs and the suitability and potential of your type of bathroom. By examining aspects of your personal and family life, such as how often you bath or shower, you will find it easier to identify the most suitable fittings and most appropriate design solutions.

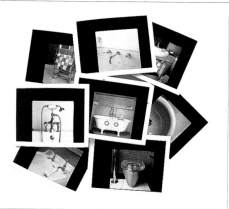

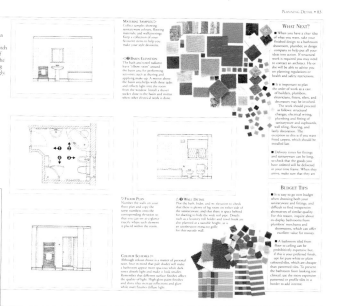
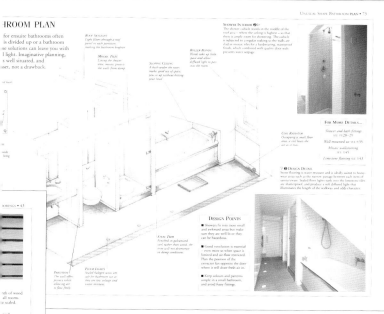

4. DESIGN YOUR BATHROOM △

When you feel satisfied with your own bathroom ideas, turn to *Plan Your Design* (*pp.76–83*), and put your design thoughts into practice. This section provides step-by-step instructions for measuring the room intended for your bathroom, plus details on how to draw the floor plan and different elevations to scale. Common design mistakes are pinpointed and successful solutions are shown and explained.

3. LEARN HOW TO PLAN △

A chapter on *Room Plans* (*pp.46–75*) looks in detail at seven existing bathroom designs and offers advice and inspiration on how to bring together all the elements in your own plan, whether you are designing a brand-new bathroom or re-modelling an existing one. A three-dimensional drawing, a bird's eye view plan, photographs, and a list of design points explain the thinking behind each of the seven design solutions.

HOW TO USE THE GRAPH PAPER

■ Draw up your room to scale (*pp.78–79*) using the graph paper provided (*pp.89–96*). You may photocopy it if you need more.

■ For a bathroom with small dimensions, use the graph paper with an imperial scale of 1:24, where one large square represents 1ft and one small square represents 3in. Or, use the metric scale of 1:20, where one large square represents 1m and a small square 10cm. Therefore, an area 60cm long is drawn across six small squares.

■ For a larger bathroom, use the imperial graph paper with the smaller scale of 1:48. The large square represents 4ft and the small squares 6in. Or, use the metric graph paper with the scale 1:50, where a large square equals 1m and a small square just 10cm.

■ Having plotted your room, try various designs on a tracing paper overlay.

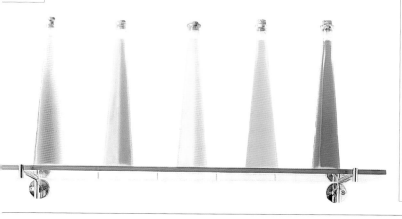

ASSESS YOUR NEEDS

THE FOLLOWING questions will help you focus on your specific bathroom needs and think about ways to approach bathroom planning so that, as you work through the book, you will be able to compile a list of the bathroom elements and designs that best suit you and your lifestyle.

BATHS AND FITTINGS

Consider the amount of time you like to spend in the bath and whether you prefer a quick dip, a long soak, or a bath that doubles up as a shower. Think about the needs of other members of the family, and whether you would like a bath that is large enough to share. These decisions will help you decide on the size and type of bath you need, plus the best fittings, and a suitable location.

■ BATHS
☐ Would fitting a corner, tapered, or compact bath free up much-needed space along one wall for an extra item of sanitaryware, such as a bidet?
☐ Do you like to spend time lying back and relaxing in the bath? If so, have you considered bath designs that will cradle your head, neck, and back in comfort?
☐ If you do a strenuous job that leaves you with aching muscles, would a spa bath system be a good idea?
☐ Do you enjoy taking a long time in the bath? If so, would you like to be sure that your chosen bath material retains the heat incredibly well? Or would a heated bath panel be useful?
☐ Would you like the bath to double up as a shower? Does the base of the bath have an anti-slip surface for safety?
☐ Is easy maintenance important to you? Remember, baths in dark colours lose their looks quickly in hardwater areas as limescale deposits mark the surface.
☐ Would you like to share a larger double bath with your partner? If so, would any structural alterations be necessary to strengthen the bathroom floor?
☐ Do you have young children or less-able family members who would find climbing in and out of a bath difficult? Would they benefit from safety features, such as grab rails?

■ BATH FITTINGS
☐ Are your children likely to pull out the bath plug? Would a pop-up waste be more practical than a plug and chain?
☐ When different members of the family take it in turns to use the bath as a shower, would a bath/shower mixer with thermostatic limiter be a wise choice to avoid possible scalding from hot water?
☐ Do you wish to be able to wash your hair over the bath? If so, have you chosen a bath/shower mixer that will suit the rim of your chosen bath?
☐ Do you have young or elderly family members who find it difficult to operate standard taps? Have you considered lever taps that are easier to use?

SHOWERS

An effective shower needs to be carefully planned to work with your existing plumbing system. Consider how many times a day you want to shower, and whether you would like to have different showering options, such as a massage setting. Think about the people who will use the shower, and whether you need safety features for the young or elderly. Also, weigh up whether it is easier to house the shower in a separate room.

☐ Do you want the convenience of instant hot water for showers at any time of the day or night or do your showering times correspond with the availability of hot water from the hot water cylinder?
☐ Do you prefer a powerful shower? If so, is it possible to install a shower pump to improve the shower's performance?
☐ If there is sufficient space, would a large, double shower, enabling you to bend and stretch without touching the sides when washing, appeal to you?
☐ Would a shower that can double up as a relaxing steam room suit your lifestyle?
☐ If you opt for a shower with body jets, can the position of the jets be altered to suit all the family members who may use it?
☐ Are there less-able members of the family who would find stepping in and out of the shower difficult, and see a built-in shower seat as a practical addition?
☐ Have you dismissed fitting a shower cubicle because space in the bathroom is restricted? Did you know that shower cubicles can be fitted with a choice of inward and sliding doors that only use space within the shower cubicle to open?
☐ Would you prefer an invigorating shower with needle jets of water, a relaxing shower with massage and pulse options, or one that offers a choice of functions to suit all members of the family?

☐ Do you like to be drenched from head to toe in water, or would an adjustable shower head be more useful that can be raised or lowered to target different parts of your body without getting your hair wet each time ?

☐ Do you like to keep soap and shampoo within the shower enclosure? Would a shower cubicle with a space designed to hold these items be useful?

BASINS AND FITTINGS

Make your choice of washbasin and fittings simple by considering the people who will be using the basin on a daily basis. Decide whether more than one person will want to have access to a basin at the same time. Will you be carrying out other activities, such as shaving and hair-washing? This will influence the height of the basin and position of the fittings.

☐ Will two people want to wash in the bathroom at the same time? Have you the space to fit twin sinks with enough elbow room for two people?

☐ Do you require space under the basin to store items? Would a wall-mounted basin help to free-up this floor area?

☐ Are you taller or smaller than average? Would it be more comfortable to fit a wall-mounted basin at a height that suits you? If so, have you checked that the wall basin you have chosen can be fitted with a syphon cover to hide the pipework or recess the supply pipes in the wall?

☐ Do you have young children who tend to overfill the basin or splash water onto the floor? Would a basin with inward-sloping edges be a good idea?

☐ Do you want to wash your hair in the basin? If so, can the spout be turned to one side so that your head can fit quite comfortably over the basin?

WCS AND BIDETS

Think carefully about who will use the wc and bidet, how often, and for how long. The most important factors are comfort and cleanliness. Other points worth considering when selecting a wc, are how easy is it to operate the flush mechanism, how much water the wc needs to flush, and whether you want a close-coupled, low-level, or high cistern wc.

☐ If you want an old-fashioned, high-level cistern, does the bathroom have tall walls to enable the cistern to sit high above the pan so that the force of water is strong enough to flush the wc properly?

☐ Does the lavatory seat rest against the cistern or wall when open to prevent it falling shut at an inconvenient moment?

☐ Will both young and old members of the household be able to sit down and stand up from the wc with ease?

☐ Would you prefer to mount the wc bowl on the wall so that the seat can be higher or lower than average?

☐ Are the contours of the wc bowl, seat hinges, water inlet, and rim easy to clean?

☐ Do you want to conserve water? Is there a choice of different flushing modes with the cistern, for example, a half press for a short flush or a full press for a long flush of water?

STORAGE

Make a mental list of the type of items you would like to keep in the bathroom. If it is a family bathroom, take account of products that will have to be stored out of reach of children. The type and amount of storage space you need to design into your bathroom will be determined by the number of products you and your family use and who requires access to these products.

☐ Do you have enough cupboard space to house your beauty and cleaning products?

☐ Could the storage of everyday items be better planned so that less-used items do not obstruct access to those you use regularly?

☐ Do you want storage cupboards that are easy to maintain in a bathroom? If so, have you checked that the cabinet finishes are steam-proof and the hinges rust-proof?

☐ Do you want a bathroom cabinet that can be locked so that medicines and cleaning chemicals can be kept away from children?

☐ Do you need a container for storing children's bathtime toys?

BATHROOM ELEMENTS

BATH SHAPES

CHOOSING A BATH that is a pleasure to use is just as important as finding one that looks good. Before coming to a decision, ask permission to climb in and out of the baths you like on your showroom visits; although you may feel ridiculous, it is the only way to make a practical choice. Once in a bath, see that it suits your body shape by stretching out your legs and reaching for the taps. Check also that fittings, such as grab rails, are well placed.

POPULAR SHAPES

The rectangular bath is still the most popular shape, partly because it fits neatly into a bathroom corner, and also because of its practical lines which enable the occupant to stretch out and lie down. From this basic shape, a range of modern space-saving designs have evolved, such as the tapered bath. For a traditional style, the old-fashioned slipper bath (*below*) or double-ended bath (*below right*) are comfortable and good-looking designs.

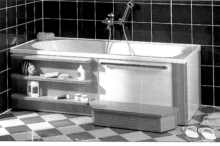

△ STANDARD BATH
The addition of a non-slip step, grab rail, and shelf unit to a standard rectangular bath are useful features in a family bathroom.

▽ SLIPPER BATH
Position freestanding baths so that there is plenty of space around them to show off their contours, and to enable you to step in and out of the bath from either side.

BATH RACK
Essential for holding washing items where wall-mounted dishes are impractical.

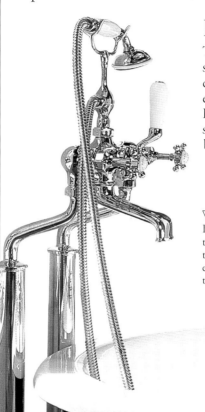

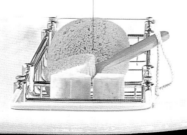

METAL SHROUDS
Tall metal cylinders conceal pipework.

BALL AND CLAW FEET
Decorative ball and claw feet hide the sturdy bolts securing the slipper bath to the floor.

OUTER SHELL
Most baths can be painted with a water-resistant paint so that they co-ordinate with the bathroom colour scheme.

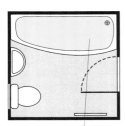

A tapered end creates space for other elements.

◁ TAPERED BATH

A clever and practical solution to cramped bathroom conditions is to install a tapered bath which gives more space where it is needed – at the end where you stand up and shower. Meanwhile, the narrow end allows space beside it for a full-size basin with elbow room; the sink can be used in comfort without hitting the bath edge.

INNER SURFACE
Enamelled surfaces are durable but colder to touch than acrylic.

ELBOW ROOM

Ensure there is room at head height to towel dry your hair.

Plan a floor area at least 90cm (36in) wide alongside the bath so that you can towel dry both the upper and lower half of your body in total comfort.

REMEMBER

■ Access to all sanitaryware plumbing is essential. Ensure that panelled bath surrounds on all types of bath can be opened quickly in an emergency by fitting either magnetic catches or hinges.

■ Abrasive cleaning liquids and chemicals can damage acrylic and enamelled bath surfaces and shorten their life. Only use products recommended by the sanitaryware manufacturer.

■ To make the bath safe for young and old people, install grab rails and non-slip mats.

△ DOUBLE-ENDED BATH

Comfortable ends and centred taps and waste are essential if the bath is for more than one. The bath should be deep enough to prevent displaced water from overflowing.

ALTERNATIVE SHAPES

Manufacturers also produce baths in circular shapes. A round or corner bath may be more in keeping with your bathing needs, especially if you enjoy sharing a bath with your partner or tend to bathe several children at once. It may fit more successfully into your room plan than a rectangular bath.

△ ▷ FULL CIRCLE

Most round baths have a greater water capacity than standard shapes so they take longer to fill up and are less economical. They are usually manufactured from acrylic or resin which makes them light, while a shelf-seat is often moulded into the design for comfort and ease of use.

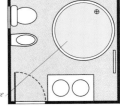

A round bath leaves space for other sanitaryware.

◁ △ CORNER BATH

A bath tucked into a corner occupies a similar floor area to a standard bath but fills the space differently, which can be an advantage when planning a bathroom layout; a corner bath is shorter than a standard bath so an extra item can be placed next to it along one wall.

This design leaves space for a radiator to warm towels.

SPECIALIST BATHS

FOR THOSE WHO PERCEIVE bathing as a special time to indulge in the therapeutic effects of water, there are a whole host of sophisticated spa systems that can both stimulate and relax you. Alternatively, you may prefer to plunge into a gleaming copper bath, or submerge yourself in a deep tub of water.

TONING AND RELAXING

The therapeutic properties of spa baths, soak tubs, and whirlpools are undeniable. They offer a perfect way to unwind at the end of the day. A stream of water mixed with air is pumped out of jets to pummel the neck, back, thighs, and feet, and encourage good circulation.

SPA BATH AND SHOWER UNIT ▷
Combining a relaxing spa bath with an invigorating shower in one compact unit makes good use of limited space. It also eliminates the need for extra pipe runs that two self-contained systems require. The circular end provides room to shower in comfort with shelves for shampoo and soaps.

WATER THERAPY
The speed of the jets can be altered for a relaxing or an invigorating body massage.

◁ **SPA BATH**
To ensure the muscles really benefit and relax, the water in the spa bath should be deep enough to lightly support the weight of the body. The water should be warm, not uncomfortably hot, to encourage a total sense of well-being.

△ **HYDROTHERAPY**
A sculptured head rest and sloping back gently support the body, aiding the jets of aerated water to massage directly along the length of the spine. A touch-control pad, within arm's reach, can alter the waterflow and also the temperature to maintain comfort levels throughout the treatment.

TEMPERATURE CONTROL
A thermostat keeps the temperature constant.

MULTI-SPRAY HEAD
Delivers a soothing pulse of water or energizing jets

NEAT PROFILE
Unobtrusive tap-heads with neat contours are less likely to be knocked.

TELEPHONE HANDSET
Traditional fittings,
mounted on the bath
rim, add character.

SIT BATHS

Sit baths take up less floor space than standard baths but keep you in an upright bathing position. Although this sounds awkward, it can be very soothing as these baths are often so deep that you can submerge yourself up to your neck in water. Taller than standard baths, they can be difficult to fit in small spaces under sloping roofs and windowsills.

◁ **HIP BATH**
Designed to be used for a quick wash rather than a long soak, a hip bath uses a small amount of space and water.

STEP DETAIL
Natural wood steps help you climb over the steep side.

SMALL PROPORTIONS
A neat shape that is suited to bathrooms where the bath has only occasional use.

DEEP TUB ▷
Two people can sit comfortably on the recessed seat in this deep tub. Finished in natural wood, the resin construction is both strong and lightweight, and the fittings are neat and unobtrusive.

REMEMBER

■ The weight of a large, full bath can be enormous. Check that the floor is strong enough to support the bath when filled with water and occupants.

■ The use of bath oils or foam is not advised in spa baths as they clog up the small aeration holes and produce a mass of bubbles. Have the jets checked and serviced regularly.

■ Wood and metal finishes require special care to ensure that they remain in pristine condition. Everyday bath cleaning chemicals are likely to damage surfaces so follow manufacturers' guidelines.

△ **WOODEN BATH**
Planks of solid hardwood are bonded together and protected with penetrating wood oil to provide a watertight seal. The moist conditions prevent the timber from drying out and so hold the planks together.

NATURAL WOOD
Clean lines and beautiful graining make a feature of this simple bath.

SPECIALIST BATH MATERIALS

Stainless steel, copper, marble, and wood can make exciting alternative materials for baths but are expensive. Unlike acrylic or resin that are warm to the touch, materials such as stainless steel, copper, and marble are cold, absorbing heat from the water and reducing its temperature. Baths can also be made from quality hardwoods. As well as being warm, they retain their heat well.

MAINTENANCE
Use a non-abrasive cleaner and soft cloth.

STAINLESS STEEL
Satin or mirror finishes are available.

△ **STAINLESS STEEL BATH**
Stainless steel bath interiors are easy to keep clean, hygienic, and hardwearing. The outer panel has been painted to give the illusion of solid veined marble.

SURFACE DETAIL
A roll top and deep sides show off the copper's gleam.

COPPER BATH ▷
The distinctive slipper shape and copper interior have classic style. The copper is protected with a lacquer finish but care must be taken not to scratch off the surface finish as blue-green staining can result.

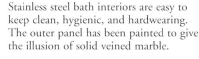

SHOWER SYSTEMS

A GOOD SHOWER IS UNBEATABLE whether you prefer invigorating needle jets of water or a relaxing massage spray. Showers use up less water than a bath, take up little space, and can be fitted into the smallest of rooms, making them ideal for busy households and as en-suite facilities. A variety of trays, together with a huge choice of enclosures and fittings, offer an infinite range of systems from which to choose.

SINGLE SHOWERS

A shower can be tailored to suit your exact requirements, from the shape and fittings to the temperature and speed at which water is delivered. Most showers are designed for one occupant with one shower head and one set of controls. Cubicle sizes vary though, so it is worth stepping inside one to bend and stretch and check that you, and other members of your family, can shower in comfort.

▽ **CIRCULAR SHOWER**
An all-in-one shower unit can eliminate the need for additional plumbing, ceramic tiling, and electrical work. Here, an overhead spray, two pairs of body jets, integral lighting, and storage for shampoos and soaps provide luxury in one compact unit.

ADJUSTABLE HEIGHT
A riser rail enables the shower head to be set at the best height and angle.

BODY JETS
Jets of water massage shoulders and legs.

TEMPERATURE CONTROLS
A pre-selected temperature stays constant when showering.

SHOWER FINISH
Low-maintenance acrylic is hardwearing and simple to wipe clean.

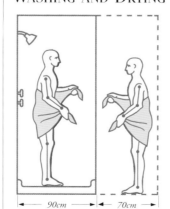

WASHING AND DRYING

90cm	70cm

It should be possible to partly dry yourself within the confines of the shower unit. You will need space to raise your arms and to bend to reach your feet.

△ **STANDARD UNIT**
A standard square shower tray will fit easily into the smallest of bathroom corners. A single shower head or combined shower head with body jets can be fitted to offer a range of showering options. Unless you choose a whole shower enclosure, a waterproof covering such as ceramic tiles must be used on the bathroom walls to prevent water penetration.

DOUBLE SHOWERS

For sharing a shower or for the luxury of having more room in which to move around, a double shower unit offers extra comfort. Most are rectangular, though round, square, and tapered designs offer flexibility when planning the layout.

▷ ▽ **ANGLED SHOWER**
The diagonally aligned shower door occupies the same area as a standard door. A roomy shower interior with multi-jet shower head, separate hand spray, and built-in seat showers one or two adults.

Doors have room to open even where space is limited.

WOODEN SEAT
A seat is useful for the less able, as well as for those taking a long shower.

△ **SHOWER ROOM**
Fully tiled walls and a central drain for waste water open out a cramped box room into a pleasant shower space. The large overhead shower rose provides a deluge of water.

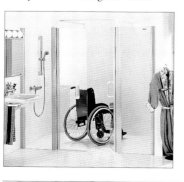

◁ **SHOWERS FOR THE LESS ABLE**
Watertight seals around the shower doors at floor level mean that less-abled users can move in and out of the shower enclosure without flooding the floor. A wide door and easily adjustable shower controls allow wheelchair access and privacy.

REMEMBER

■ Where space is limited, showers can be fitted under the stairs or on a landing.

■ Arrange quotes for the plumbing, tiling, and electrical work, and include these in your budget when working out the total price of the installation.

■ Check first with your installer that the system you intend to buy is compatible with your water supply.

■ Shower trays come in four materials: steel, acrylic, resin or composite, and ceramic. Run your hand over the materials to decide which one you prefer.

SHOWER SURROUNDS

Keeping the rest of the room dry and enjoying the benefits of an effective shower relies on containing the water within the showering space by means of a screen, door, or curtain. The least expensive option is a waterproof curtain, while the most expensive is a toughened glass surround.

△ **SHOWER CURTAINS**
PVC and plasticized fabrics used for modern shower curtains are impregnated with fungicide to prevent mildew.

SHOWER DOORS ▷
In the event of breakage, shower doors manufactured from tough safety glass shatter like a car windscreen into thousands of pieces that cause little harm.

△ **STANDARD**
Hinged on the left or right, the doors open into the bathroom.

△ **INFOLD**
Made in two sections, the door folds into the shower cubicle so that it does not take up any floor space.

△ **PIVOT**
Partly opening into the unit, the door occupies little space.

◁ ▽ **SHOWER POD**
Space and light are the main features of this spectacular shower room, constructed from toughened frosted glass. Stainless steel handles are used to slide the doors open and closed. A wood floor and central shower rose add to the pleasure of the experience.

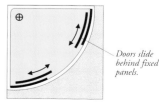

Doors slide behind fixed panels.

SHOWER AND BATH FITTINGS

GOOD QUALITY FITTINGS are as important as the sanitaryware itself. Many bathrooms are bought with the taps and wastes included in the price. As well as complementing the bathroom style, they should be durable and easy to operate – even with soapy hands. Shower, bath, and tap fittings are used many times throughout the day, so invest time choosing the right details to ensure that even the most economic of bathrooms is a pleasure to use.

BATH SHOWER MIXERS

Bath shower mixers are fitted with a "divertor" handle that can be switched over to fill the bath or to operate the shower. They are ideal for washing your hair and rinsing out the bath after use, and are indispensable if there is no room in the house for a self-contained shower unit.

◁ **FIXED SHOWER**
A decorative swan-neck riser with a fixed shower rose is ideal if you prefer a total soak rather than a light shower. The slender pipework remains static once in place, so you must supply a precise measurement for the shower height, to ensure that you will be able to stand upright under the shower rose.

FIXED ROSE
The jet of water cannot be adjusted.

SHOWER CRADLE
The hand-held shower allows freedom of movement.

△ **RETRACTABLE HANDSET**
These telescopic hoses fit neatly within the bath surround and slide in and out for use. They are less likely to catch against other fittings as the shower hose is tidied away. Not all bath shower mixers are available with retractable handsets.

SHOWER HOSE
Flexible for a full-height shower or for rinsing the bath.

SHOWER SUPPLY
Try to buy all three elements of a fixed shower from the same supplier to ensure that they match.

SHOWER HEAD
Set at a fixed angle, the spray cannot be adjusted.

"DIVERTOR" HANDLE
Choose a handle that automatically returns to fill the bath after a shower to prevent accidental scalding.

◁ **TELEPHONE HANDSET**
In general, telephone handset designs fit standard baths where two tap-holes have been punched into the bath rim. However, some traditional handsets are available from specialist bath shops for non-standard baths and for baths that have been recessed into a fixed surround, such as marble.

TAP CROSSHEAD
Traditional design with the benefits of modern technology.

CERAMIC HANDLE
The "divertor" should move easily but feel secure when located in either the bath or shower position.

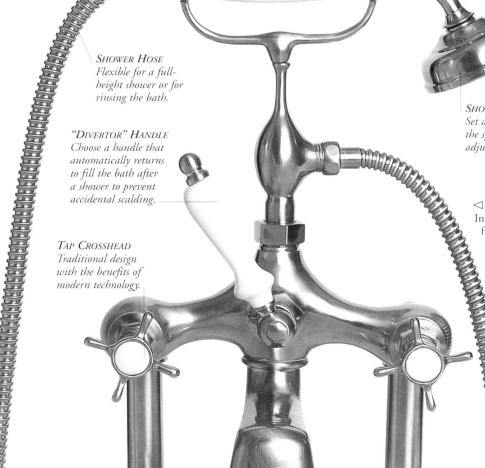

SHOWER FITTINGS

A shower must maintain a good flow of water at a constant temperature. Before purchase, check that the controls respond quickly and have built-in safety features to avoid scalding. Always check with the installer that the type of shower you want to purchase is compatible with your water supply.

◁ **THERMOSTATIC CONTROL**
Thermostatic shower controls are fitted with a shut-off valve to control the water flow and maintain a constant temperature. The heat can be adjusted by mixing different volumes of hot and cold water.

HOSE
The pipe is reinforced to prevent buckling that will restrict water flow.

ELECTRICALLY HEATED ▷
An electric shower is connected to both the mains water and electricity supplies, and only heats water when it is needed, making it very economical.

SELF-CLEAN
By twisting the rim, small filaments push through the spray holes to eject limescale.

△ **DIRECTIONAL HEAD**
A fixed head is attached to the wall and the pipework is hidden from view. The angle of the shower head can be altered to suit any user, while the spray options range from relaxing pulses to invigorating needle jets.

BAR CONTROL
Hot and cold water inlets deliver a pre-set temperature of water to the shower head.

REMEMBER

■ Single-control thermostatic valves are easy to use by just turning the lever or dial from the off position through cold, warm, and then hot.

■ Dual-control thermostatic valves regulate the water flow and keep the temperature constant. Anti-scald devices are available which cut off over a hot but bearable 38°C/100°F.

■ Try out plumbed-in shower heads and fittings in bathroom showrooms to see how simple they are to operate.

■ When buying antique taps and fittings, check that they will work with your sanitaryware.

BATH FITTINGS

Many bath taps in manufacture have the latest ceramic disc technology, enabling taps to be turned on or off fully with just a quarter turn. Ceramic discs have a hard, polished surface creating a watertight seal and drip-free "off" position. They also work well in hard water areas where limescale can build up around taps, making them difficult to operate.

△ **RIM-MOUNTED TAPS**
These are fitted to the edge of baths that usually have pre-drilled tap-holes. All have a larger feed and water flow capacity than basin taps.

△ **WALL-MOUNTED PILLAR TAPS**
A combined tap-head and spout direct the flow of water. The spouts need to be sufficiently long to extend over the rim of the bath.

△ **WALL-MOUNTED MIXER TAPS**
Two taps and a central spout are wall mounted at the end of the bath or on one side. The plumbing is chanelled into the wall to hide it.

△ **WATERFALL SPOUT**
A wide band of water cascades into the bath and offers a neat, almost flush finish. Mixer taps keep the water temperature consistent.

WASTE

Dirty water from the bath, shower, bidet, and basin will drain out through the waste where a simple filter catches soap deposits and hair that can then be removed periodically to prevent a blockage in the pipes. Wastes and bath taps are often sold as a package to ensure they match one another.

△ **POP-UP WASTE**
Modern pop-up wastes are often operated from the tap mounting where a simple lever is lifted or depressed to open or seal the waste outlet. Their smooth surface is unobtrusive and comfortable if touched, and cannot be accidentally pulled out when bathing.

PLUG AND CHAIN
This traditional system is still popular and sold with the waste fitting.

BASIN TYPES

MOST WASHBASINS are supported on a pedestal or fitted within a countertop or washstand. These arrangements work well to conceal the plumbing, but the basin is set at a fixed height which can be a disadvantage if you are taller or shorter than average. A wall-mounted basin, however, can be attached to the wall at a height that suits you.

PEDESTAL BASINS

Available in a huge variety of styles and sizes, pedestal basins usually stand 85–90cm (34–36in) high. If you need even more height, you can raise the pedestal by standing it on a platform. Install the basin before fixing a splashback to the wall behind to ensure that the basin will not interfere in the design.

INTEGRAL STORAGE ▷
The space beneath a basin is a useful place to hide toiletries that are not used on a day-to-day basis and to store bathroom cleaning equipment. As well as boxing in the pipework, a well-designed below-counter unit can become an interesting feature in its own right and contribute to the character of the bathroom. Open storage areas in bathrooms are best kept for attractive bath products and accessories (see p.31 and pp.36–37).

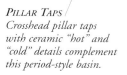

PILLAR TAPS
Crosshead pillar taps with ceramic "hot" and "cold" details complement this period-style basin.

SWAN-NECK SPOUT
A high spout offers easy access to the washing bowl.

MIXER TAPS
Hot and cold water temperature and flow can be mixed with precision.

OUTER EDGE
A high outside rim keeps the water within the basin.

SLIM PEDESTAL
A pedestal makes it easier to stand close to the basin.

△ **STANDARD MODEL**
Traditional ceramic pedestals are bolted to the floor and sometimes to the bathroom wall for stability. Pedestals provide additional support for the basin and hide any unsightly pipework.

ASYMMETRIC BASIN
The platform for resting a bar of soap adds both an element of interest and practicality to this freestanding design.

REMEMBER

■ Natural wood should be treated regularly with a coat of penetrating wood oil to repel water splashes and to maintain its distinctive graining. Warmth from bathroom radiators and heated towel rails can cause warping, so place wood items away from these elements.

■ Most manufacturers of ceramic sanitaryware offer a choice of pedestal, countertop, or wall-mounted basins, and also smaller or larger than standard basin sizes.

■ Marble countertops can stain so wipe up spills immediately and buff with a soft cloth to avoid permanent damage.

COLOUR DETAIL
A gloss-painted pedestal, a smooth ceramic basin, and a wooden storage unit, make a durable and eye-catching arrangement.

STORAGE SPACE
The maple wood storage unit opens to reveal freshly laundered towels.

TOE SPACE
Feet can be tucked under for closer access.

BASIN SIZE

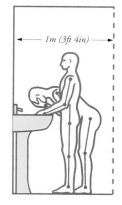

1m (3ft 4in)

Choose a basin that fits the space comfortably and leaves plenty of room to lean over and wash your face or brush your teeth without knocking into the wall behind.

WALL-MOUNTED BASINS

These space-saving basins simply need fixing to a solid wall or upright that can take the weight of the basin when it is full of water. The waste outlet is hidden within a simple syphon cover or a cylindrical "bottle-trap" (*right*). Free space beneath the basin makes the bathroom feel larger, and it can store bathroom weighing scales or a stool.

◁ **NEAT FIT**
The clever use of space means corner basins can be tucked into the smallest of rooms. Choose taps very carefully; large fittings will take up up too much of the wash area.

GLASS BASIN ▷
A wall-mounted basin is simple to fasten to the wall at your own waist-height for ease of use (*see also p.33*).

(see also p.33)

WASHSTANDS AND DOUBLE BASINS

Traditional and modern washstands offer a range of facilities within one unit: basin, worktop, storage, shelving, and access to plumbing. The basin can be centred within the washstand with a countertop on either side, or placed off-centre to provide a larger uninterrupted worktop for keeping make-up or shaving equipment close at hand.

△ **DOUBLE BASINS**
Twin basins solve the problem of two people wanting to wash at the same time. A mirror running the length of the wall above the marble countertop and cupboards ensures that users do not get in each other's way.

WOODEN RAIL
Towels can be draped over the rail making a separate towel rail unnecessary.

ACCESS COVER
A removeable plate means that plumbing is easy to reach in an emergency.

△ **OPEN STORAGE**
Natural wood, frosted glass, stainless steel, and wicker add interest and character to this open-fronted washstand. Simple accessories and white towels keep the look fresh and uncluttered, while semi-opaque drawers mean that stored items are not forgotten but stay dust-free.

SHELF SPACE
An open shelf creates space for large and small items.

△ **COVERED STORAGE**
Utilitarian items including toilet paper and cleaning materials are kept to hand but are hidden from view. The cupboards are fitted with adjustable shelves for extra flexibility.

BASIN FITTINGS AND MATERIALS

THE CHOICE OF BASIN MATERIAL can add an interesting new dimension to your overall bathroom design as many basins are now moulded in a variety of exciting shapes from specialist materials. When judging which fittings and surface finish best suit your household needs, take into account your family's washing habits, and how many times the basin is used morning and night.

DECK-MOUNTED TAPS

The ledge or rim of most basins has pre-drilled tap-holes which conform to a standard 3.6cm (1⅛in) diameter. Whichever style of basin you choose, there is usually a one tap-hole, two tap-hole, or three tap-hole version to fit any tap combination be it a single-lever tap, a pair of pillar taps, or a three-piece basin mixer. When choosing, remember basin taps are smaller than bath taps.

COLOUR CODED
Blue for cold and red for hot make tap covers easy to interpret.

△ **EASY-ACTION ATTACHMENTS**
Conventional taps often require several turns to operate fully, and can be difficult for the less able and children. Attachments such as these can be gripped and twisted more easily.

△ **PILLAR TAPS**
Basin pillar taps fit into a pre-drilled two-hole basin. These widely spaced pillar taps allow room to bring your head right down to the basin when washing your face or brushing your teeth.

WHITE CERAMIC
Simple lines and a smooth finish create a clean, crisp style.

△ **BASIN MIXER**
Period-style ceramic handles operate the basin mixer to blend hot and cold water. The three-piece mixer set is designed for a three-hole basin.

MONOBLOC TAP
The monobloc mixer tap delivers water at the desired temperature.

▽ **SINGLE LEVER**
Monobloc basin mixer taps fit into a single tap-hole, taking up much less basin space than two- or three-piece taps. The main advantage of this design is the smooth, easy-to-operate lever that controls the flow and temperature of the water from the tap.

LEVER ACTION
A slim, "pen-like" lever is simple to manoeuvre.

CHROME FINISH
A chromium-plated finish reflects other colours in the room.

NATURAL FINISH

Wood may seem like an unusual choice of material for a basin but the water-resistant properties of marine plywood make it a good choice if you prefer something a little different. The ply has been cleverly moulded into shape by steam to form a sinuous line, then cut to provide a smooth ledge for storing basin accessories. A back panel protects the wall behind from splashes of water.

◁ **SINGLE LEVER**
Like other basin mixer taps, this simple design takes the guesswork out of running and mixing water to a comfortable temperature. The pipework is recessed, so that the basin can be set closer to the wall.

▽ **DOUBLE LEVERS**
The distinctive "pepper mill" style levers have bulbous ends to help you grip and turn them even when wet. The position of the spout is fixed so water falls directly into the basin.

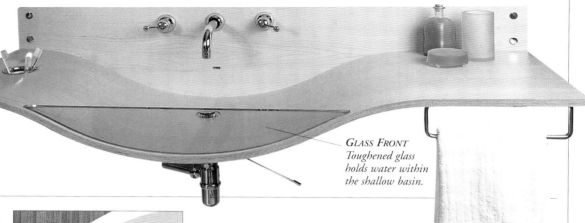

GLASS FRONT
Toughened glass holds water within the shallow basin.

BASIN MATERIALS

Ceramic basins are still the most popular choice, though the use of metal and glass designs are becoming more widespread. Marble, granite, wood, and mineral resin compounds can be custom-made to suit specific requirements but are expensive. It is also worth noting that basins set within a counter or washstand must be well fitted with the basin edge sealed to prevent water and damp from penetrating the surrounding unit. Deep, inward-sloping rather than shallow basin rims will help to protect the countertop area from stray splashes of water.

△ **POLISHED BRASS**
To prevent discoloration, solid brass is highly polished and the surface coated with a protective finish that resists water and scratching. Non-abrasive cleaners and buffing with a soft cloth maintains the lustre.

△ **RECONSTRUCTED MARBLE**
Powdered marble is mixed with resin and coloured to create a compound that feels as smooth as marble but is much stronger and stain-resistant. Numerous finishes can be chosen from plain to veined marble effects.

△ **TOUGHENED GLASS**
Thick safety glass is durable and scratch-resistant. It is shown off to best advantage when fixed on discreet brackets or a block of wood.

△ **STAINLESS STEEL**
Mirror polished stainless steel looks good with contemporary chrome taps. It wipes clean easily and is hygienic but the mirror finish can scratch so opt for a brushed stainless steel finish for heavily used basins.

COLOURED FINISHES
Soap deposits are visible on coloured basins.

CERAMIC ▷
Hardwearing and very easy to clean, ceramic basins are available in a range of colours to match any other item of sanitaryware.

WCs AND BIDETS

THE NEED FOR FRESHNESS, cleanliness, and hygiene dictates the most suitable materials for wc and bidet manufacture, though the designs can be as aesthetically pleasing as other items of sanitaryware. The need for water-conservation has been the driving force behind the latest designs, which combine style with environmentally friendly water-saving flush mechanisms.

VISIBLE CISTERNS

Most wcs have a cistern which is both visible and easy to access in emergencies. The cistern is usually placed flat against the wall, either above or directly behind the bowl. Elaborately ornate 19th-century cisterns can be bought independently of the bowl but, on the whole, the cistern is purchased as part of the wc suite, and includes the cistern lever or handle and flush mechanism.

◁ **CLOSE-COUPLED WC**
These wc suites are made with the cistern and bowl attached, giving the most compact of all wc designs. The cistern rests on a ledge or platform at the back of the bowl and is also secured to the bathroom wall with sturdy mountings.

SLIMLINE CISTERN
A narrow cistern allows the wc bowl to be butted up close to the wall, so that it takes up no more space in the bathroom than is absolutely necessary.

SMOOTH EDGES
The seat follows the line of the bowl and does not overlap the edges.

EMBOSSED PANEL
A decorative panel hides ugly plumbing from view.

PULL CHAIN
Ceramic, wood, and metal handles can be chosen to match other fittings.

FLUSH PIPE
To look their best, chrome, brass, or gold-plated finishes should be mirror-polished.

HIGH-LEVEL CISTERNS ▷
If you wish to install this type of wc, check that the room is tall enough; the cistern needs to sit high above the bowl, where it is connected by a long length of pipe, to create enough force for a proper flush. High-level cisterns can be noisy but new technology has produced quieter models.

REMEMBER

■ A high-level cistern requires sturdy mountings to withstand the force applied to the flush, and a strong wall to support the weight of the water in the cistern when it is full.

■ WCs with either high-level cisterns or tall panel-style cisterns will only really fit on an uninterrupted wall space, otherwise the flush pipe or cistern height is likely to obstruct bathroom windows, dado rails, or cornicing.

■ WCs and bidets need to be kept scrupulously clean, so choose models with smooth, curved lines where every area is accessible. Select wc seats with well-spaced hinges so that you can clean between the gaps.

■ The recommended position for using a standard height wc is leaning forward with your feet tucked slightly back to emulate a squatting position.

GOOD POSTURE

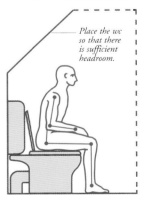

Place the wc so that there is sufficient headroom.

The wc bowl should be low enough for your feet to rest flat on the floor when sitting. There should also be headroom for a man to stand upright.

WCs with Hidden Cisterns

Back-to-wall and wall-mounted wcs both use a cistern that can be installed behind a false wall or panelling so that only the flush lever remains visible. The cisterns are usually plastic and set at a minimum height of 80cm (32in).

BACK-TO-WALL WC ▷
With germ-harbouring surfaces hidden away, back-to-wall designs are both hygienic and unobtrusive. Manufactured in brushed stainless steel, the bowl is easy to keep clean, while the adjacent floor and wall area can just be wiped over, making this a good choice for busy family bathrooms.

PRISTINE FINISH
Stainless steel is less likely to stain and take on odours.

◁ WALL-MOUNTED WC
Unlike back-to-wall wcs, wall-mounted designs sit above floor level. The weight of the wc and the person sitting on it has to be borne by the wall and mountings alone. Wall-mounted wcs work well in small bathrooms as they keep the floor area free and easy to clean.

COMFORT FACTOR
With wall-mounted designs, you can have the bowl fixed at a height that suits you.

Personal Hygiene

Bidets are an invaluable aid to personal hygiene. Place them alongside the wc so that they can be used after going to the wc. They should be comfortable to sit on, so take care to choose a bidet with a curved rather than angular rim, and one that is wide enough to support both thighs and bottom.

BIDET MIXER
The directional nozzle also makes rinsing out the bidet much easier.

PEDESTAL BIDET ▷
Bidets mounted on pedestals are also useful for washing feet or the dirty hands and knees of young children. For this reason, it is practical to have towels close at hand and a non-slip floor surface where splashes can be quickly wiped up.

STRONG DETAIL
Select a bidet with a solid pedestal and a chunky outline for classic good looks.

◁ WALL-MOUNTED BIDET
Wall-mounted designs keep the bathroom floor clutter-free so that it can be kept scrupulously clean. The raised rim also prevents water from spilling onto the floor, while the colourful tap-heads introduce a novel element to the functional.

WC Seats

Seats come in many finishes, but standard fittings mean that they can be fastened to most wc bowls. Ideally, the wc seat should have a raised rim at the back so that when you are seated, the body is tilted forward into the squatting position.

△ LESS-ABLED SEAT
This specially designed seat raises the level of the rim so that it is easier to sit down.

◁ FAMILY SEAT
Smaller members of the family tend to slip through adult-sized wc seats. This flexible adaptor has both a child seat and an adult seat. It helps to make time spent toilet training easier.

◁ POLISHED WOOD SEAT
A wooden seat is often more comfortable than plastic and feels warm. Here, carved out "leg spaces" support the thighs.

JAZZY SEAT ▽
A new range of wc seats made from colourful laminated plastics livens up the wc.

BOLD COLOURS
Try a fun approach with amoeba shapes and vivid colours.

STORAGE

SPACE FOR STORING a range of products is often limited in bathrooms, but if it is well planned you can have shelves and open units to display attractive bottles and jars, plus areas behind closed doors for utilitarian items, such as toilet tissue. Here medicines can also be hidden from view, and out of reach of small children.

△ OPEN STORAGE TROLLEY
A three-tiered trolley stores towels, toiletries, hair-grooming equipment, and cosmetics where they can be seen. It is easily moved to the activity area where the products are needed. Check that the trolley can glide across the floor and that the drawers do not stick.

FREESTANDING STORAGE
Bathroom cabinets and shelf units that stand alone take up valuable floor space which can be a problem in small rooms. If this is the case, look for a cabinet that is raised above the floor so that items can be tucked underneath or select a unit with glass shelves which will look lighter.

STATIC STORAGE ▷
Take advantage of spaces where sanitaryware will not fit to place a tall storage unit. Towels, soaps, and accessories can be attractively displayed.

COMPARTMENT SPACE
Items kept within closed compartments are less susceptible to dust.

STORAGE HEIGHT

Items taken out frequently, to use morning and night, should be kept at the front of a wall cabinet, somewhere between waist-height and eye-level. Bulkier items, such as towels and cleaning equipment are best kept on lower shelves.

△ CLOSED STORAGE TROLLEY
If you prefer closed storage, a trolley with some covered units may be more useful so that bottles and jars of varying heights will be able to fit within the confines of the sections.

ADJUSTABLE HEIGHT
Shelf heights can be easily adjusted to suit the items you wish to display.

WALL STORAGE

Apart from areas taken up by windows and doors, blank walls in small bathrooms present marvellous storage opportunities. Shelves and wall cabinets leave floor areas clear, and every item can be stored within arm's reach, just above or below eye-level. Try to avoid deep shelves so that items do not become lost or forgotten at the back.

◁ **OPEN SHELVES**
Gradated shelf units – where the lowest shelf is shallowest – will not obstruct the bathroom occupant at shoulder-height. Choose a style that is easy to keep clean and dust-free.

FROSTED GLASS
Less decorative items are hidden behind a semi-opaque door but can be identified.

STREAMLINE SUPPORTS
Glass shelves and slimline brackets do not clutter up the limited wall space.

◁ **CUPBOARD STORAGE**
A mix of everyday items on display will clutter up countertops and look unsightly. Hide them from view by storing them in an attractive cabinet with a child-proof safety lock.

REMEMBER

■ A bathroom can reveal a great deal about its owner. If you share it with others or visitors are likely to use it, keep your personal products hidden from view to avoid embarassing yourself or your visitors.

■ Mirrored cupboard fronts often have magnetic catches, making handles unnecessary. This leaves a clear, reflective area that gives the impression of additional light and space.

■ Piles of neatly folded towels look great in a bathroom but they need to be kept fresh and aired or they will become damp and start to deteriorate.

UNDERCOUNTER STORAGE

In compact bathrooms, built-in basins and freestanding washstands with storage space beneath the sink area make good sense. Shelves should be easy to slide in and out so that you can adjust their height at will, as most toiletries, cosmetics, and toilet tissue vary enormously in size. It is also advisable to place very small items in containers so that they do not fall out every time you open the door. Access to plumbing under the basin is vital, a leak in this storage area could ruin items, such as cotton wool.

TAP FEATURE
A pop-up waste mechanism is fitted under the basin.

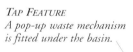

BASIN DESIGN
A shallow basin sits neatly on top of the conical pedestal.

◁ **UNDERCOUNTER CUPBOARDS**
Melamine-faced units are easy to clean and can withstand knocks in bathrooms subject to heavy traffic. Use plastic containers to keep delicate items, such as cotton-wool, dust-free.

BOTTLE SAFETY
A rail holds bottles in place and prevents them from falling out when the door is opened or closed.

PEDESTAL STORAGE ▷
A contemporary freestanding basin balances both aesthetic and practical needs. The conical-shaped pedestal tapers to the ground so that it occupies less floor space, and is fitted with storage shelves.

HEATING AND VENTILATION

NOTHING DESTROYS THE PLEASURE of a warming bath or shower more than having to step back into a cold room or dry yourself with damp towels. Wet skin is particularly sensitive to a drop in temperature, so heating and ventilation are important considerations when designing the room to make time spent in the bathroom, particularly during the colder winter months, an enjoyable part of your daily routine.

FREESTANDING HEATING

Radiators are the easiest and most widely used method of heating a bathroom because they are virtually maintenance-free. Other freestanding options – which look fabulous in traditional bathrooms – include coal-burning stoves and gas-fired fuel-effect designs. Both of these need adequate ventilation to prevent condensation.

BALL JOINTS
For a classic touch, choose high-polished finishes and ball joints.

△ **HEATED TOWEL RAIL**
Useful for drying out and warming up towels, most heated rails should not be relied upon to heat the bathroom too. Install a wall radiator as well for this purpose.

COLOUR OPTIONS
Special heat-resistant paint finishes have been formulated for use on radiators.

HEAT EFFECTIVE
Column radiators have a greater output than panel radiator designs.

△ **COLUMN RADIATOR**
Most bathrooms are heated by radiators linked to the central-heating or hot-water system. Column radiators are effective heaters and work well in retro-style bathrooms. Alternatively, neat bathroom storage heaters can be installed to work on cheap-rate electricity.

AIR CIRCULATION
Leave space under and around the radiator to enable warm air to circulate.

METALLIC FINISHES
The rail is available in brass, chrome, and nickel finishes to match existing bathroom fittings.

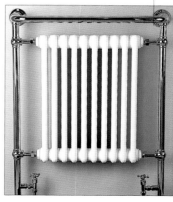

△ **RADIATOR TOWEL RAIL**
If you only have space for one heater, choose a combination radiator that works in conjunction with your heating system and also has a rail for warming towels. Place the radiator so towels can be in easy reach of the bath or shower.

SPACE-SAVING HEATING

It is surprising how much wall space a radiator or heated towel rail occupies – space that could well be used for an additional item of sanitaryware or storage. Several discreet, dual-purpose heaters are now on the market that will fit into the smallest of spaces. Some can be incorporated into the bath panel while others fit into the kickspace under a storage unit.

◁ **HEATED PANEL**
Panelling around baths is purely cosmetic, but some manufacturers produce a low surface temperature panel that will also keep bath water warmer for a longer period.

△ **WALL HEATER**
A fan heater will provide warmth within moments of being switched on. Look for additional features, such as a choice of speed and heat settings, and a shaver socket.

TOWEL SPACE
Make sure that the spaces between the rails can hold the largest of your towels.

◁ **PLINTH HEATER**
Take advantage of "dead" space under bathroom units by installing a plinth radiator. The slim panel design is connected to the existing hot-water central-heating system, and also works as a fan during the summer months. Booster settings will rapidly take the chill off a bathroom as the hot air rises from ground level to warm the room.

△ **HEATED SHELF**
Towels placed on the shelf are kept warm and aired with a heater element. Placed directly below a bathroom mirror, the heater element will also reduce misting and condensation.

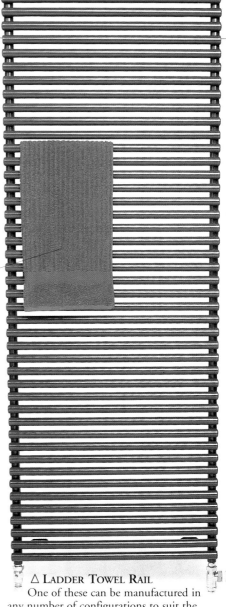

△ **LADDER TOWEL RAIL**
One of these can be manufactured in any number of configurations to suit the wall space. They are finished in heat-resistant metallic or plain colours. Towels can be hung at a height that is practical for the user.

VENTILATION SYSTEMS

Good ventilation is required in bathrooms because insulation and double-glazing are so effective in modern homes that moisture-laden air does not disperse after a hot, steamy bath or shower. Instead, the moisture condenses on the walls causing damp and mould growth, as well as fabrics to rot and wallpaper to peel.

◁ **LIGHT EXTRACTOR**
A build-up of steam in a shower cubicle tends to block out the light. To overcome this problem, install a low-voltage ceiling light in the shower unit. Choose a system that has a built-in extractor fan to suck away the steam.

△ **HEAT RECOVERY**
A heat exchanger saves 80 per cent of heat that is expelled into the air with moisture; it transfers heat from warm out-going air to cold incoming air.

AIRFLOW IN A BATHROOM

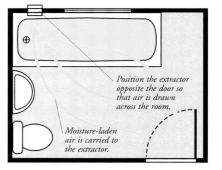

Position the extractor opposite the door so that air is drawn across the room.

Moisture-laden air is carried to the extractor.

Fitting an extractor fan to the outside wall is a simple way to expel air quickly from the room and reduce steam and condensation; ducting is a more complicated alternative.

LIGHT SOURCES

WELL-THOUGHT OUT LIGHTING and your choice of window treatment will contribute enormously to the character of the bathroom. Consider accent lighting to highlight key areas, mood lighting for a soothing atmosphere, or bright, functional lighting for a family room, but bear in mind that water and electricity are a lethal mix, and so the fittings you select must be safe. Your choice of window treatment has no such limits but should provide both privacy and style.

PLANNED LIGHTING SYSTEM
Diffused lighting casts a soft background illumination; accent lighting focuses on the basins.

POINTS TO CONSIDER

■ Safety features are of paramount importance when selecting lighting for bathrooms. Ensure ceiling lights are sealed within a glass or plastic steamproof diffuser. Waterproof bulkhead lights – designed for garden use – work well in bathrooms, particularly showers, where the shower doors reduce the light level. Even though bulkheads are waterproof, always fix them high on the wall or overhead where they cannot be accidentally knocked or drenched by water from the shower head.

■ Fluorescent lighting gives a clear, shadowless light but can look cold and harsh in bathrooms. Reduce the glare by placing fluorescent tubes behind a diffuser panel. Bathroom cabinets are often fitted with fluorescent lights to throw light on the countertop below.

■ Good lighting will make it easier to perform intricate bathroom activities, such as applying cosmetics and shaving. It can also highlight hazardous wet areas on the floor where you could slip.

■ Bathroom lights are usually switched on and off by a pull cord inside the bathroom or by a switch outside the room to prevent water from coming into contact with the mains electrical supply.

WINDOW TREATMENTS

OPAQUE GLASS

This glass can be plain, or have a textured, acid-etched, or sandblasted finish, to echo the bathroom theme.

ADVANTAGES
• Obscures the view from passers by.
• Makes curtains or blinds unnecessary.
• Allows maximum daylight to filter through.

DISADVANTAGES
• Hand-finished designs can be expensive.
• Can look cold and clinical.
• Does not retain heat in winter.

LIGHTING

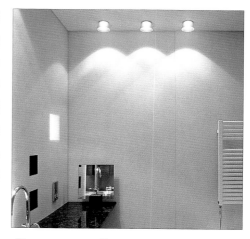

OVERALL LIGHTING

A central light or several downlighters will cast an even light over the whole room but can lack imagination and may be unsuitable for task areas.

ADVANTAGES
• Simple to plan and install.
• Casts an even light over the room.
• Wide choice of styles and fittings available.

DISADVANTAGES
• Uniform lighting is not always interesting.
• Shows up imperfection on walls and ceilings.
• Angles difficult to adjust.

ROLLER BLINDS

Offering a limitless choice of colours, patterns, and textures, roller blinds draw attention to the window area.

ADVANTAGES
- Easy to fit.
- Take up a minimum amount of space.
- Huge choice of colours and designs.

DISADVANTAGES
- Block out light if you want daytime privacy.
- Difficult to clean and dust.
- Some spring mechanisms can jam in use.

CURTAINS

These add interest and colour, they emphasize your taste and style, and frame an otherwise plain window.

ADVANTAGES
- Can co-ordinate with the colour scheme.
- Make bathrooms look less cold and clinical.
- Retain heat within the room.

DISADVANTAGES
- Dust and steam can damage the fabric.
- Opening and closing can be disruptive.
- Can be expensive.

SHUTTERS

Slatted shutters maintain privacy without blocking out the natural light. Their simple style works well in bathrooms.

ADVANTAGES
- Slats can be angled to let in daylight.
- Can be finished in natural wood or colours.
- Take up little space.

DISADVANTAGES
- Are usually custom-made and expensive.
- Slats can be difficult to clean.
- Humid bathrooms may cause wood to expand.

DIFFUSED LIGHTING

Non-directional lighting offers a soft, ambient atmosphere that is successful in both hi-tech and traditional bathrooms where a relaxed environment is desired.

ADVANTAGES
- Has a relaxing effect.
- Can disguise less than perfect surfaces.
- Reduces glare from mirrors and white fittings.

DISADVANTAGES
- Cannot be used for task lighting.
- Can be expensive.
- May need additional light sources.

TASK LIGHTING

Bathroom activities performed in front of a mirror, such as putting in contact lenses, need task lighting to provide a direct, clear source of light.

ADVANTAGES
- Can be directed where required.
- Boosts light in otherwise gloomy areas.
- Can be wall- or ceiling-mounted.

DISADVANTAGES
- May bounce off white surfaces causing glare.
- Provides an unflattering light for complexions.
- Throws strong shadows.

AMBIENT LIGHTING

A soft light transforms a bathroom by creating a warm and tranquil setting in which to relax. Candle-light is the most atmospheric with its flickering glow.

ADVANTAGES
- Disguises surface blemishes.
- Offers a soft, all-round calming light.
- Makes bathing and showering an event.

DISADVANTAGES
- Several candles are needed to cast enough light.
- Cheap candles can produce plumes of smoke.
- Candles must be set away from fabrics for safety.

FLOORINGS

STEAM, SPLASHES, WET FOOTPRINTS, spilt creams and lotions all take their toll on bathroom floorings so choosing a suitable material needs careful thought. Before coming to a decision, consider each flooring material in terms of durability, comfort, hygiene, and aesthetic appeal. Carpets, for example, are soft and comfortable to tread on with bare feet, but deteriorate in damp conditions, while ceramic tiles are hardwearing but cold underfoot. Weigh up the pros and cons of each to avoid a costly mistake.

HAND-COLOURED TILES
A highly imaginative use of colour turns a patchwork of tiles into a kaleidoscope of tones.

MARBLE

Marble flooring has a timeless quality, making it a desirable choice for both contemporary and traditional bathrooms.

ADVANTAGES
• Low maintenance and hardwearing.
• Natural beauty does not deteriorate with age.
• Smooth surface will not harbour dust or dirt.

DISADVANTAGES
• Slippery when wet and may stain.
• Expensive to buy and fit.
• Requires a strong sub-floor below.

LINOLEUM

A natural material that presents some of the most versatile options in creative flooring. Custom-made floor patterns are designed with the aid of a computer.

ADVANTAGES
• Extremely hardwearing.
• Good for allergy sufferers; it will not hold dust.
• Warm and quiet underfoot.

DISADVANTAGES
• More expensive than most vinyl floorings.
• Must be laid by an experienced fitter.
• Can crack if the sub-floor is not level.

POINTS TO CONSIDER

■ No matter how good the flooring you choose, incorrect fitting or laying will result in an uneven surface that will wear badly. Always have the flooring installed by a professional fitter as most guarantees will be invalidated if the material is laid incorrectly.

■ Unless laid by an expert, the weight of a ceramic, stone, or marble floor on top of wooden floorboards may cause the floor to sag. Also, wood expands and contracts with changes in warmth and humidity, so tiles may crack or grout fracture. A plywood sub-floor must be fitted to ensure that the floor remains stable.

■ Strong detergents and abrasive cleaners can ruin highly polished or vinyl floor coverings, producing discoloration on pale surfaces and the appearance of matt patches. Always check the manufacturer's instructions for the best method of cleaning.

■ Bear in mind that busy or large floor patterns may overpower the rest of the bathroom, especially if the room is small and the suite and fittings are plain.

■ Natural coir matting is well suited to bathrooms as the fibres benefit from being kept moist, but it can be prickly on bare feet.

CERAMIC TILES

Hardwearing and impermeable, these tiles can take a good deal of punishment and are available in a wealth of colours.

ADVANTAGES
- Low-maintenance and almost indestructable.
- Widely available and relatively inexpensive.
- Produced in neutral, pastel, and primary hues.

DISADVANTAGES
- Slippery when wet, and cold underfoot.
- Noisy when walked on in shoes.
- Grouting can be difficult to clean.

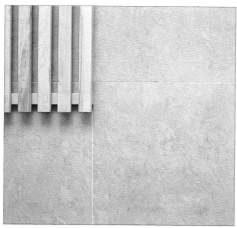

LIMESTONE

Along with other natural stones, pale grey limestone has a characteristic grain and texture that improves with age.

ADVANTAGES
- Natural colour blends with all bathroom styles.
- Easy-to-clean surface.
- Extremely hardwearing.

DISADVANTAGES
- Expensive to buy and install.
- Cold to walk on barefoot.
- Slippery when wet.

WOOD

The colour, grain, and warmth of wood make it a popular choice in all rooms but bathroom floors must be sealed.

ADVANTAGES
- Plank or stripwood is simple to install.
- Mellows and improves with age.
- Works well in modern and traditional settings.

DISADVANTAGES
- Needs regular maintenance to look its best.
- Water penetration can swell and lift planks.
- Noisy when walked on in shoes.

VINYL

The most inexpensive and widely used type of floor covering, produced in both sheet and tile form. Designs range from plain finishes to textured marble.

ADVANTAGES
- Inexpensive and easy to lay.
- Warm, soft, and quiet underfoot.
- Hardwearing and waterproof.

DISADVANTAGES
- Ripples appear if laid on an uneven surface.
- Discolours if exposed to sunlight.
- Damaged by heavy furniture or shoe heels.

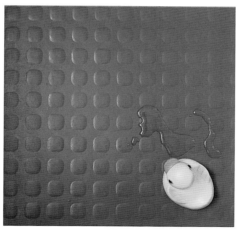

RUBBER

Stud rubber flooring is available in sheet or tile form. It is both hardwearing and water-resistant; many architects choose it for commercial buildings.

ADVANTAGES
- Virtually indestructable.
- Quiet and warm to walk on.
- Waterproof surface has anti-slip finish.

DISADVANTAGES
- Expensive to buy.
- Only stocked by specialist floor suppliers.
- Must be installed by an experienced fitter.

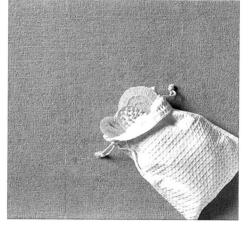

CARPET

Probably the most popular type of floor covering as it provides comfort and warmth, and prevents noise from an upstairs bathroom reaching downstairs.

ADVANTAGES
- Available in sheet or tile form.
- Limitless range of colours, patterns, and piles.
- Prices to suit all budgets.

DISADVANTAGES
- Steam and water cause jute backings to rot.
- Requires regular vacuuming to maintain look.
- Underlay must be fitted to give good wear.

WALLCOVERINGS

THE MATERIALS YOU CHOOSE to furnish the walls in bathrooms can vary from zone to zone. Shower and bath areas take the greatest punishment so wallcoverings chosen for these "wet" areas must be able to stand up to a soaking several times a day and be easy to wipe clean. For other more general areas of the bathroom, paint or wallpapered finishes may be more appropriate but even these wallcoverings must have a washable finish and be specially treated to restrict mildew in the humid bathroom environment.

PAINT

Specially formulated bathroom paints have a washable vinyl finish. They also contain fungicides to restrict mildew.

ADVANTAGES
• Inexpensive to buy.
• Quick and easy to apply.
• Infinite range of colours available.

DISADVANTAGES
• Paint marks, so splashbacks are also needed.
• Looks dull if used on large expanses of wall.
• Not tough enough to be used in shower areas.

HARDWORKING WALLS
Architectural glass bricks allow light to penetrate, while mosaic tiles are durable and easy to clean.

CERAMIC TILES

A range of tile colours, patterns, and sizes are now produced that are suitable for all bathroom areas including the shower surround.

ADVANTAGES
• Easy to clean.
• Heat resistant and waterproof.
• Reasonably priced.

DISADVANTAGES
• Must be fixed to sound walls or may crack.
• Square tiles can look monotonous in large areas.
• Grouting can attract dirt and mildew.

POINTS TO CONSIDER

■ Exterior bathroom walls are colder and so more prone to condensation. Select an insulating wallcovering, such as a vinyl, or a paint specially formulated for bathrooms or kitchens to reduce the problem.

■ High walls can make a small bathroom appear cold and clinical. Balance the proportions of the room by selecting one colour for lower walls and a co-ordinating colour for the upper walls. Profile tiles fixed at picture rail height can create an effective horizontal break in a large area of wall, as can wood mouldings that have been stained or painted.

■ Pale colours make bathrooms appear lighter and more spacious. Choose large mirrors placed opposite natural light sources to give the impression of additional space.

■ Paint is the most versatile and inexpensive of wallcoverings and offers the opportunity to experiment with a wide range of finishes from sponging to stencilling. The effects and colours can be selected to achieve total co-ordination.

■ Look for a wallcovering that features a complementary colour in its design or opt for one that contrasts with the sanitaryware you have chosen to install in the bathroom.

WALLPAPER

Vinyl finishes are best for bathrooms, last longer, and give a bathroom a more furnished, comfortable appearance.

ADVANTAGES
• Readily available and inexpensive.
• Easy to hang.
• Wide range of colours, patterns, and finishes.

DISADVANTAGES
• Can hide fungal growth behind the paper.
• May peel or bubble in humid conditions.
• Thin paper may show up wall imperfections.

TEXTURED PLASTER

Rough plaster is a fashionable finish but it must be sealed in bathrooms to prevent water penetrating the surface.

ADVANTAGES
• Masks uneven wall surfaces.
• Requires no special skills to apply.
• Is a durable and inexpensive finish.

DISADVANTAGES
• Rough plaster attracts dust and dirt.
• Can scratch bare skin.
• Cannot be used in shower area.

WOOD PANELLING

Useful for boxing in a bath and covering up uneven walls, wood panelling must be sealed to make it water-resistant.

ADVANTAGES
• Easy to install even for the amateur.
• Inexpensive and widely available.
• Can be painted or stained to your specification.

DISADVANTAGES
• Cheaper softwood panels can dent if knocked.
• Damp may cause the wood to warp.
• May not suit all styles of bathroom.

MOSAIC

Available in sheet form for ease of use, mosaic tiles are extremely durable and water-resistant, making them ideal for shower enclosures and splashbacks.

ADVANTAGES
• Adds character and interest to all surfaces.
• Easy to lay.
• Offers interesting design opportunities.

DISADVANTAGES
• Intricate designs are time-consuming.
• Grout can harbour soap and dirt.
• Can look municipal if used over large areas.

GLASS BRICKS

Ideal as a screen where natural daylight has to be "borrowed" from another living area, glass bricks look best in contemporary spaces.

ADVANTAGES
• Add an area of interest.
• Are extremely durable and waterproof.
• Allow light to filter through.

DISADVANTAGES
• Expensive.
• Need to be installed professionally.
• Can make a bathroom appear cold.

GRANITE

A natural stone, granite comes in a range of tones. It is ideal for splashbacks and is best kept to small areas, especially dark stone which can look hard and cold.

ADVANTAGES
• Hardwearing and low maintenance.
• Easy to clean.
• Can enhance the simplest bathroom suite.

DISADVANTAGES
• Expensive.
• Requires expert installation.
• Can be cold against the skin.

ROOM PLANS

FITTED BATHROOM PLAN

ALL BATHROOMS BENEFIT from good planning as key items of sanitaryware have to be fitted into a limited area without the user feeling cramped. A fitted design capitalizes on every available space from floor to ceiling. All pipework and ducting is boxed in, and slim storage units are shoe-horned into narrow spaces. Mosaic and melamine offer durable finishes in bold colours and present simple, clutter-free surfaces in both wet and dry areas.

SLIM UNIT
A fitted cupboard, set between the windows at eye-level, stores soaps, shower gels, and shampoos close to the bath.

Fitted bath *Wall-mounted wc* *Mosaic counter*

INTERNAL ROOM
DIMENSIONS:
2.4m (7ft 8in) wide
2.7m (8ft 8in) long

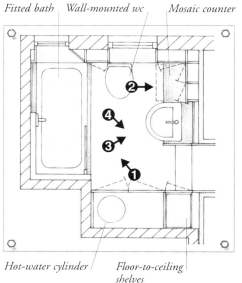

Hot-water cylinder *Floor-to-ceiling shelves*

△ BIRD'S EYE VIEW
Windows above the bath and wc filter daylight into the room. The wc is against the outside wall for access to the soil pipe. Other items are built in so as not to obstruct movement in the room.

OPTICAL ILLUSION
A wide, sloping sill balances the small window frame with the larger one next to it.

SANITARYWARE
A white bath, wc, and basin look clean and simple within this bold colour scheme.

△ ❶ BATH SURROUND
The back wall is just long enough for a full-sized bath to be fitted against it. Dazzling blue mosaic tiles provide a hardwearing, waterproof surface for the back wall and bath edge, while a mirror fitted into the recess reflects light from the window keeping the area bright and open.

AWKWARD RECESS
A recess, too narrow for shelves, is put to good use with a large, light-reflecting mirror.

FOR MORE DETAILS...

Wall-mounted wc SEE P.35

Wall storage SEE P.37

Opaque glass SEE P.40

Mosaic tiles SEE P.45

BATH SURROUND
Mosaic provides a waterproof ledge on which to place washing items.

❷ SMALL DIVISIONS ▷
Most bathroom products are
packaged in small containers and
tubes, so individual cupboards
divided up by shelves keep them
tidy, easy to find, and less likely
to become lost or forgotten.

DISCREET CUPBOARDS
Personal items and medicines
are hidden behind push-open
panels without handles.

BASIN HEIGHT
A semi-countertop
basin is sunk into
the surface so that
the basin sits at a
suitable height.

FLOOR-TO-CEILING
STORAGE
A slim unit with
adjustable shelf
heights stores
bathroom towels
and toilet tissue.

△ **❸ SPACE SOLUTIONS**
The basin is off-set to the right of the fitted units to
provide a large area of mosaic worktop to the left on
which to place items in use. The orange panelling beneath
the basin neatly conceals the plumbing and has space for
storing essential bathroom cleaning materials. To the left
of the basin, a large wooden linen box slides open to
collect dirty laundry. Like the rest of the cupboards, there
is no handle on the linen box to interrupt the simple,
fitted look; instead it opens by placing your finger into
the cut out "finger-hole". The mirror magnifies the room
making it appear much larger than it actually is.

NON-SLIP STAIRS
Steps leading down
to the bathroom are
trimmed with a
non-slip edge to
prevent accidents.

AIRING CUPBOARD
Decorative holes in the
plywood doors allow air
to circulate around the
hot water cylinder inside.

DESIGN POINTS

■ Strong blocks of colour work
best where there is plenty of
natural daylight to maintain
a fresh, spacious environment.

■ Marine plywood can be used
throughout bathrooms as it is
water-resistant. Alternatively,
use standard plywood and coat
the natural wood finish in
yacht varnish; this will protect
it from water splashes and
humidity which can cause the
wood to warp.

■ Back-to-wall wcs and bidets
require panelling to hide away
the pipework and plumbing
mechanics of each item. This
often creates storage space
within the area boxed in, and a
top edge that serves as a useful
shelf for accessories.

△ **❹ PRACTICAL MATERIALS**
All the surfaces have been constructed out of materials
that suit bathroom conditions, are inexpensive, and
are readily available; water-resistant paint finishes for
the front of the units and window surrounds, plywood
for the airing cupboard, and mosaic. The result is an
interesting and original fully fitted bathroom.

FITTED BATHROOM CHOICE

△ WALL-TO-WALL VENEER

A rich veneer clads the walls, cupboards, and drawers to produce a uniform effect which ensures the back-to-wall wc panel and varying height units blend unobtrusively. Sets of drawers contain toiletries and accessories, leaving surfaces clear for decorative items. Areas that could become wet or marked are finished in marble, which is both practical and attractive.

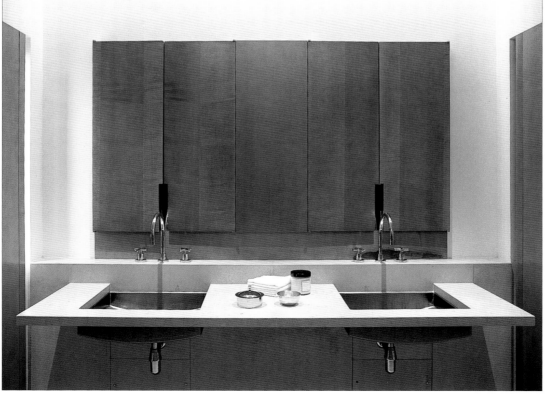

△ FITTED HEATING

Primrose-yellow panelling is chosen throughout the bathroom to make it appear brighter and larger. Fitted units and open shelves make good use of space below the basin, and a panel heater in the "kickspace" makes a wall radiator unnecessary.

◁ LESS IS MORE

Simple chrome fittings ensure that the beauty of the natural wood and marble can be fully appreciated. The two basin recesses, cut out of a marble worktop, echo the straight lines and symmetry of the wall cupboards. Diffused lighting reflects in the wall-to-wall mirror.

MARBLE SIMPLICITY ▷

A single sheet of pale grey marble is fitted along the length of the left wall with a basin set to one end to maximize the countertop area. The same finish is applied to the end wall and the bath surround, creating continuity as well as an attractive hardwearing surface; spillages must be wiped up or marble may stain.

UNFITTED BATHROOM PLAN

UNLIKE FITTED BATHROOMS where cabinets fill every space from floor to ceiling, the unfitted plan takes a more relaxed approach. Here, furnishing the bathroom like a boudoir with a comfortable armchair and other pieces of furniture, not usually associated with bathroom design, is encouraged. With a large bath as the focus, this room becomes a special place in which to unwind.

WINDOW TREATMENT
A plain roller blind softened by drapes provides warmth, style, and privacy.

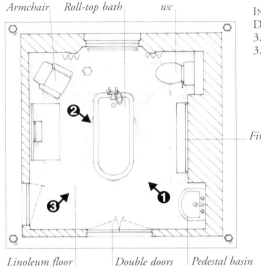

Armchair   Roll-top bath   wc

INTERNAL ROOM
DIMENSIONS:
3.2m (10ft 4in) wide
3.5m (11ft 4in) long

Fireplace

Linoleum floor   Double doors   Pedestal basin

△ BIRD'S EYE VIEW
The bath sits in the middle of the room in front of a traditional cast-iron fireplace. An alcove to the left of the fireplace houses a close-coupled wc; the alcove on the right has a pedestal basin.

△ ❶ ROLL-TOP BATH
A beautiful piece of furniture in its own right, an antique roll-top bath can be placed at any angle in the room because the plumbing is concealed within metal shrouds that rise up from the floor. This bath has been positioned in front of the fireplace and makes a wonderfully bold focal point.

ARMCHAIR
A big comfortable chair provides a place to relax following a luxurious bath.

CHEST OF DRAWERS
Towels and toiletries are stored in deep drawers, while cosmetics, brushes, and a mirror sit on top.

FIREPLACE
The coal-burning fire creates a cosy, intimate atmosphere when lit.

ANTIQUE DETAIL
A mahogany wall shelf adds to the "furnished" look of the room.

DESIGN POINTS

■ Unfitted bathroom designs also work with contemporary sanitaryware and furniture.

■ Exploit architectural features, such as alcoves and fireplaces to add extra character to the room.

■ Details, such as pictures, fresh flowers, and candles, contribute to the "furnished" look.

■ Polish wooden furniture to protect it from bathroom humidity and water splashes which cause wood to warp.

△ ❷ PERIOD STYLE
The alcove to the right of the fireplace is large enough to accommodate a full-sized pedestal basin with "elbow room" and wall space above for a shelf and cabinet. Brass taps and other fittings have been chosen to reinforce the period theme. The deep ochre painted walls create a warm backdrop for the white sanitaryware and pale fireplace surround, and also show off the mahogany furniture to best advantage.

SHELF UNIT
A brass gallery shelf displays a selection of bottles and jars.

△ ❸ BATHING ATMOSPHERE
The importance of lighting for setting the atmosphere in a room is often under-estimated. Here, the roll-top bath and other pieces of furniture are lit by the warm glow of the candle-light and firelight which creates a soothing environment for bathing. For some, candle-light may seem an impractical choice. Low-voltage halogen downlights operated from a dimmer switch (outside of the room) may offer a more practical solution; halogen downlights are both neat and unobtrusive, and will cast a bright light for everyday tasks.

FOR MORE DETAILS...

Freestanding bath SEE P.22

Pedestal basin SEE P.30

Linoleum flooring SEE P.42

Roller blinds SEE P.44

FLOOR DETAIL
Cut to resemble a period tiled floor, linoleum provides warmth underfoot.

UNFITTED BATHROOM CHOICE

△ CLEAN LINES
Diagonally placed sanitaryware offers an interesting alternative layout. The bath's position contrasts with the horizontal lines of the windows and doors in the adjacent room, while the monochromatic colour scheme creates a strong visual link, and gives a sharp, clean-cut look to this stylish bathroom.

△ SET PIECE
A large limed oak linen press with panelled doors and raised cornice is the focal point of this traditional bathroom. The press is placed on a wall opposite the bath, so that the fresh towels and toiletries are only a few steps away. The freestanding clothes horse, washstand, and large oval mirror create an air of elegance.

◁ CLASSIC COMFORT
Dark wood and antique furniture turns this bathroom into an informal, comfortable room that blends easily with the classic sanitaryware and flooring. A weeping fig tree in the corner has architectural proportions and creates a natural screen between the bathroom and the bedroom, when the adjoining doors are open.

FUN AND FUNCTION ▷
Acres of space in this warehouse flat allows an adventurous bathroom layout. There are no hard partitions or walled-in areas to inhibit one's movement. When privacy is needed, an area can be divided off with a striped screen. Two stainless steel washstands and a clever division of space mean that more than one person can use the room at once.

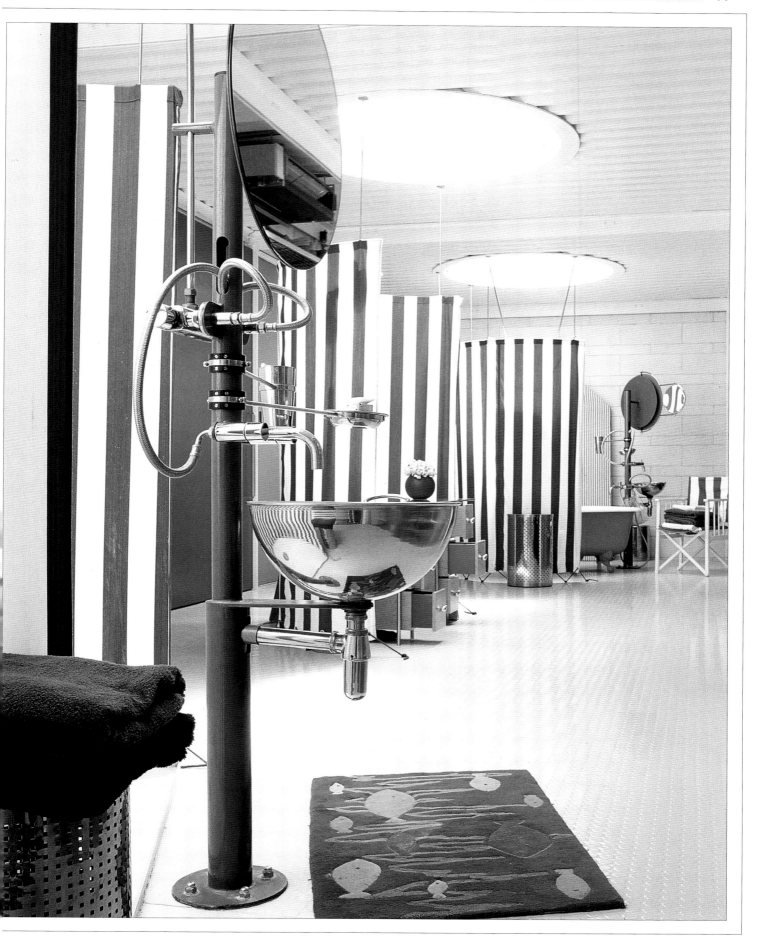

IMPROVISED BATHROOM PLAN

EVEN WITH LIMITED FUNDS, it is possible to apply the ergonomic
principles of bathroom design and produce excellent results.
Rather than pulling out your existing sanitaryware
and starting from scratch, assess what you
like and dislike about the bathroom.
Perhaps by just changing the lighting
or bath and basin fittings you can create
a space that is a pleasure to use.

Low-level wc   *Fitted bath*

OPAQUE GLASS
*Inexpensive to fit, opaque
glass offers privacy and
a modern finish.*

◁ **BIRD'S EYE VIEW**
This narrow bathroom contains
a rectangular bath, pedestal
basin, and wc, with enough
space between each item to use
them comfortably. It benefits
from a large window on the end
wall that lets in natural light.

Basin

Linen basket

**INTERNAL ROOM
DIMENSIONS:**
1.5m (4ft 9in) wide
3.1m (10ft 1in) long

△ ❶ **WORKING SPACE**
If existing sanitaryware is in good condition, there is no need
to change it. Replacing small details, such as the seal around
the bath and renewing or whitening tile grouting can make
all the difference, giving a room a new lease of life.

LOW-LEVEL WC
*The original low-level
wc remains against the
exterior wall. The pipes
have been repainted to
give them a fresher look.*

FOR MORE DETAILS...

Basin fittings SEE P.32
Overall lighting SEE P.40
Linoleum SEE P.42
Ceramic tiles SEE P.44

LINOLEUM TILES
*New buff-coloured tiles
are laid on a hardboard
base; they must be glued
down well or water may
cause them to lift.*

PAINT FINISH
Specially formulated
bathroom paint is
inexpensive and reduces
the chance of condensation
and mildew forming.

MIRRORED CABINET
A cabinet that doubles up
as a mirror offers a budget
solution to storing products
used on a daily basis.

DESIGN POINTS

■ Unless the plan of the bathroom can be improved, leave the sanitaryware where it is, as removing it could cause unnecessary expense.

■ Updating the bath and basin fittings alone can transform the look of sanitaryware at a fraction of the price of a complete refit.

■ New white grouting can improve the look of old tiles.

■ New blinds and curtains divert attention from a dull view.

WALL TILES
Half-tiled walls
provide a durable
waterproof surface
where needed.

△ ❷ NEW TECHNOLOGY

Old taps and fittings lose their mirror brightness over time and limescale builds up on the surface making them look permanently dirty. Tap-holes are pre-drilled to a standard size, so it is simple to replace old bath and basin taps with new ones that have the latest technology (*see p.29*). Plugs, chains, and wastes can also be changed.

△ ❸ IDEAS IN ACTION

A central ceiling light has been removed to make way for chrome halogen downlights which are low-voltage and operated by a pull-cord, so safe to use in bathrooms. Arranged in pairs, the lights accentuate areas over the bath, wc, basin, and doorway. A mirror-fronted cabinet and long mirror on the opposite wall also help bounce light around the room. As an inexpensive alternative to a combined radiator towel rail (*see p.38*), a chrome rail has been fixed over the panel radiator so that towels can be warmed while the room is being heated.

LINEN BOX
A wooden linen box adds
style and can also double
up as a bathroom stool.

IMPROVISED BATHROOM CHOICE

△ BRIGHT DESIGN

Plain white tiles are inexpensive and widely available. When teamed up with brightly coloured ceramics, paint, and towels, the finished effect is fun and upbeat. Here, old cabinet doors have been replaced with fabric to match the ceramics.

STENCILLED STARS ▷

If it is not within your budget to change the design of your bathroom to suit your needs, transform its appearance by stencilling the walls, floor, and ceiling. On a larger budget, clever wood panelling and lighting can make a huge difference.

◁ MEDITERRANEAN UPDATE

Painting the bathroom is one of the least expensive ways to instantly improve its appearance. Here, deep blue and sea foam colours make a focal point of the white bath, while a beachcomber's hoard of stones and pebbles, arranged under the bath, create an artistic finishing touch.

▽ FRESH APPROACH

Keep existing sanitaryware but clad the bathroom walls in tongue and groove panelling, painted white for a fresh look. A budget wallcovering, it helps to conceal uneven walls and ceilings. A new wc seat and taps help update old sanitaryware.

△ OLD FASHIONED FITTINGS

One way to improve a large bathroom on a restricted budget is to buy sanitaryware and fittings from an architectural salvage yard. Although supplies are not guaranteed, a hand-decorated wc, roll-top bath, and fittings can be bought for less than the cost of modern reproductions.

DUAL-PURPOSE BATHROOM PLAN

A LARGE, LUXURIOUS BATHROOM where space is given over to activities other than bathing can make good planning sense. Obvious partnerships include a bathroom-cum-dressing room where you can wash, dress, and groom yourself in privacy, or a bathroom and fitness room where you can shower after exercising, or taking a sauna.

Roll-top bath   *Wardrobes*   *Dressing table*   *Shelves*

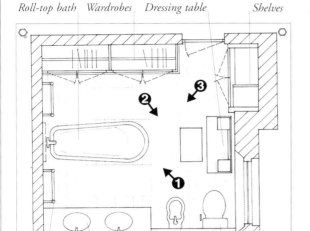

Towel rail   *Double basin*   *Bidet*   *wc*

△ BIRD'S EYE VIEW
The bath sits in the centre of the room well away from the fitted wardrobes, shelves, washbasins, dressing table, wc and bidet. All the facilities are well spaced around the large room so that a sense of order prevails.

INTERNAL ROOM
DIMENSIONS:
3.5m (11ft 4in) wide
3.6m (11ft 7in) long

HANGING SPACE
Clothes are hung up while hats and shoes are stacked on shelves above and below.

PANELLED DOORS
The lower section of the doors are panelled to match the other walls.

METAL SHROUDS
Chrome-plated cylinders cover the pipework.

◁ ❶ SURFACE DETAIL
All the surfaces – wall panelling, door fronts, and floorboards – are painted in the same low-sheen paint finish so that they are both durable and waterproof. The wardrobe doors are panelled to look like the walls and are fitted with self-closing magnetic catches so that they are unobtrusive when closed.

STORAGE
Shelves beneath the double basin store toiletries and cosmetics.

❷ DUCTED PLUMBING ▷
The lower section of the walls around the bathroom are clad in tongue and groove panelling. Behind the wc and bidet the panels are brought forward to box in the pipework required for the sanitaryware.

NATURAL LIGHT
The dressing table and mirror are situated close to the window to benefit from natural light.

DRESSING TABLE
Small drawers next to the mirror store cosmetics and beauty products close to hand.

CENTRAL HEATING
A large room such as this needs to be well-heated. A grille provides an attractive and safe cover for the large radiator.

WALL SPACE
Lining up a low-level wc, bidet, and basin unit, leaves wall space above for a mirror and painting.

DESIGN POINTS

■ Leave access points in the panelling where pipework can be easily reached for any essential maintenance.

■ Painted floors can be slippery when wet so choose a suitable low-sheen finish, and provide cotton mats with non-slip backings to absorb splashes.

■ When a bath sits in the middle of a room, supply a bath rack for soap and sponge.

FOR MORE DETAILS...

WCs and bidets
SEE PP.34–35

Heating and ventilation
SEE PP.38–39

Wallcoverings SEE P.44

❸ LIGHT AND SPACE ▷
Every activity area is carefully placed so that it is just a few steps from the main activity – bathing. From the bath you can reach out and take a towel from the heated towel rail, and step out of the bath on either side to dry yourself in comfort. From here, it is just a few steps to the basin to continue your routine before getting dressed.

DUAL-PURPOSE BATHROOM CHOICE

△ BATHROOM-CUM-SITTING-ROOM
Space beneath the window has been fitted with a sofa and plenty of cushions, to create a comfortable, quiet place in which to relax and read a book or magazine. It also enables other family members to sit in and catch up on the day's events with the bath's occupant.

▽ BATHING UNDER THE EAVES
This converted attic space remains open plan so that the pitched ceiling and beams can be fully appreciated. Separate zones have been allocated for a breakfast and dressing table, while the bath occupies centre stage.

△ CLOTHES-WASHING IN STYLE
Partitioning off a section of the bathroom to install a washing machine makes good use of the existing plumbing. For the washing area to be an attractive addition to the rest of the bathroom, the machine alcove and storage shelves are painted a vivid blue.

SIMPLE RELAXATION ▷
Two floor levels in one room present the opportunity to create a special bedroom-cum-bathroom. The close proximity of the bath to the bed makes it easy to slip effortlessly from one to the other, which is particularly enticing when you are tired or simply want to relax.

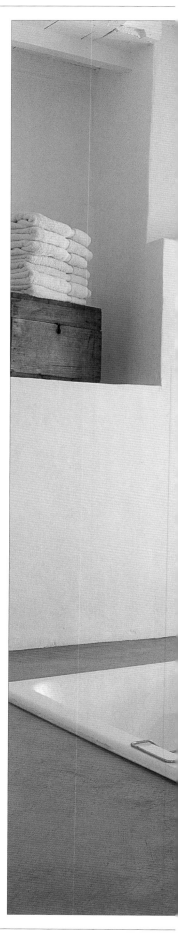

CHILDREN'S BATHROOM PLAN

CREATING A BATHROOM for young children which is both fun and safe to use is simple as long as you are aware of a few basic principles when planning and fitting the room. For example, fit child-proof locks to cupboards, ensure there are no sharp edges around the bath and basin area, choose a non-slip flooring, and have plenty of water toys to keep the users happy.

CHILD'S SEAT
Bolted on to a standard size wc, the small seat can be replaced when the child is older.

Standard bath   *Storage*   *Part-enclosed wc*   *Wall shelf*

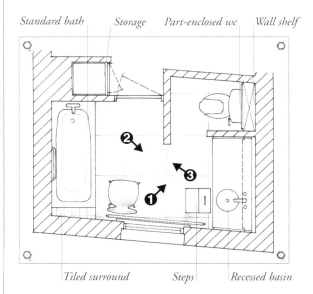

Tiled surround   *Steps*   *Recessed basin*

△ **BIRD'S EYE VIEW**
The bath and basin sit flush against the walls so that no element juts out which may be knocked. The wc area is screened off but accessible, and steps help children reach the basin.

INTERNAL ROOM DIMENSIONS:
3.2m (10ft 4in) long
2.5m (8ft 1in) wide

SHOWER HEAD
Children tend to dislike showers, so a friendly dinosaur head helps to make this activity fun.

△ ❶ **PRIVATE CORNER**
The partitioned-off wc area offers a degree of privacy for young children but because there is no door, they cannot accidentally lock themselves in. Intended for children learning to use a grown-up wc independently, this allows adults to easily help if the child needs it.

FOR MORE DETAILS...

WC seats SEE P.35

Storage SEE PP.36–37

Heating and ventilation SEE PP.38–39

Rubber flooring SEE P.43

TILED SURROUND
Grouted ceramic tiles will sustain a regular soaking and are hardwearing.

❷ USING THE BASIN ▷
Brushing teeth or washing hands can be difficult when taps are hard to reach. A step that will not topple over and can be moved around as required will encourage children to perform their morning and bedtime routine independently.

WALL CUPBOARDS
Choose a unit that locks to keep toiletries and medicines out of children's reach.

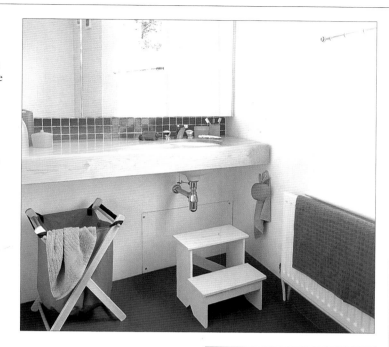

COUNTERTOP
Rounded edges and an easy-clean finish are essential.

LAUNDRY BIN
A brightly coloured fabric laundry bin can be tucked under the countertop, out of harm's way.

DESIGN POINTS

■ Provide a laundry bin to encourage children to deal with their dirty clothes rather than leaving them strewn all over the bathroom floor.

■ A cold bathroom will make children grumble and resist baths; warmth, fresh towels, and water toys will go a long way to overcoming their dread.

■ Flooring should be chosen for its resistance to accidental spills and splashes, and should be soft and warm enough for children to walk on barefoot.

WOODEN STEPS
Choose a sturdy but light design that children can move into place.

CHAIR
Install a chair for adults supervising bathtime and towel-drying children sitting on their lap.

BATH SAFETY ❸ ▷
To make bathtime as safe as possible for young children, choose a bath with a curved edged so that little hands can get a grip when climbing in and out of the bath. Fit a brightly coloured grab rail for children to hold on to when standing up in the bath, and place a rubber mat on the enamelled bath bottom to make it less slippery.

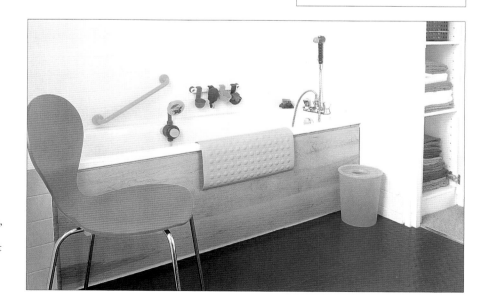

CHILDREN'S BATHROOM CHOICE

△ DEVELOPING SKILLS
With the help of your children, paint murals on ceramic bath tiles to make bathtime fun. Use cold ceramic paints that are easy to apply and durable once fully dry.

◁ FUR EFFECT
Add a touch of humour by painting a cow print or tiger print on the side of the bath. Alternatively, a mix of bright colours, spots, and squiggles will make it fun to use.

△ CUT-OUT CREATIONS
Cut-out superheroes and TV characters bring instant colour to bare walls, while red rubber flooring and red wc seat, blind, and pipework appeal to children. Colour-coded plastic jars keep soaps and sponges tidily.

3-D DESIGN ▷
Clever ideas transform this colourful bathroom into an underwater kingdom children will treasure. All the decorative surfaces are varnished so that they are waterproof and can be wiped clean when necessary.

SHARED BATHROOM PLAN

COMMUNAL BATHROOMS with a shower, a bath, and a double basin unit need not be very large but they must be well planned. There should be space around the sanitaryware so that the user does not feel too cramped, and a plentiful supply of hot water to feed the shower, bath, and basins so that they can be enjoyed by different members of the family at the same time. An efficient heating and ventilation system to heat the room and extract steam is also essential.

◁ **❶ CORNER DETAIL**
This discreet area, tucked around the side of the shower, is practically planned: the bottom shelves keep toilet tissue next to the wc, while a warm radiator warms towels which are easy to reach when you step out of the bath.

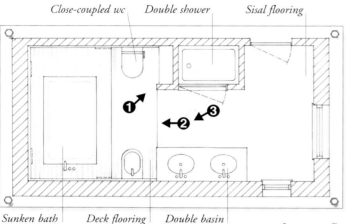

Close-coupled wc   Double shower   Sisal flooring

Sunken bath   Deck flooring   Double basin

△ **BIRD'S EYE VIEW**
In this large room, two runs of sanitaryware sit opposite one another along the walls; the double basin and bidet are placed opposite the shower and wc. The sunken bath, set within a cedarwood platform, at the far end of the bathroom, creates an inviting focal point.

INTERNAL ROOM
DIMENSIONS:
2.7m (8ft 8in) wide
5.5m (17ft 9in) long

GLASS SHELVING
Space left at the side of the shower is fitted with glass storage shelves.

WALL LIGHTS
Sealed lights are waterproof and shatterproof, making them an ideal choice for this setting next to the bath.

LIFT-UP SECTIONS
A tiled surface below the decking means that the wood planks can be lifted out and the area beneath cleaned.

◁ **❷ EFFECTIVE LIGHTING**
The simplicity of this two to four person sunken bath benefits from its bright position beneath a clear glass skylight which can be opened wide on bright days. At night, a far more subtle lighting effect is achieved by recessed wall lights; these cast a soft glow for relaxing, intimate evenings.

SCENTED WOOD
When splashed with water, the cedarwood releases a fabulous woody aroma.

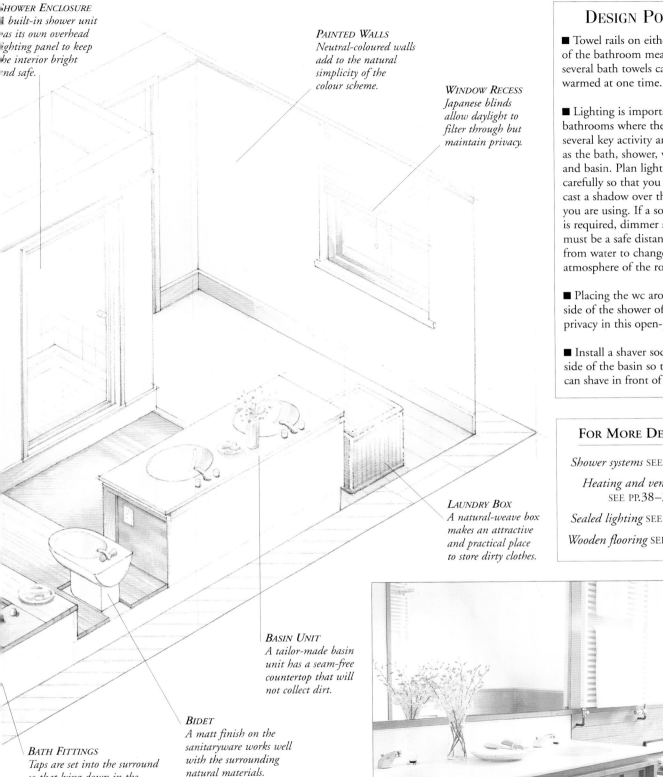

SHOWER ENCLOSURE
*A built-in shower unit
has its own overhead
lighting panel to keep
the interior bright
and safe.*

PAINTED WALLS
*Neutral-coloured walls
add to the natural
simplicity of the
colour scheme.*

WINDOW RECESS
*Japanese blinds
allow daylight to
filter through but
maintain privacy.*

LAUNDRY BOX
*A natural-weave box
makes an attractive
and practical place
to store dirty clothes.*

BASIN UNIT
*A tailor-made basin
unit has a seam-free
countertop that will
not collect dirt.*

BIDET
*A matt finish on the
sanitaryware works well
with the surrounding
natural materials.*

BATH FITTINGS
*Taps are set into the surround
so that lying down in the
bath is more comfortable.*

DESIGN POINTS

■ Towel rails on either side of the bathroom mean that several bath towels can be warmed at one time.

■ Lighting is important in bathrooms where there are several key activity areas, such as the bath, shower, w.c, bidet, and basin. Plan lighting carefully so that you do not cast a shadow over the area you are using. If a softer light is required, dimmer switches must be a safe distance away from water to change the atmosphere of the room.

■ Placing the wc around the side of the shower offers a little privacy in this open-plan room.

■ Install a shaver socket on one side of the basin so that you can shave in front of the mirror.

FOR MORE DETAILS...

Shower systems SEE PP.26–27

Heating and ventilation
SEE PP.38–39

Sealed lighting SEE PP.40–41

Wooden flooring SEE PP.42–43

SCREENED STORAGE ❸ ▷

A combination of wipe-clean surfaces, subtle colours, and natural wood create a low-maintenance room and a tranquil setting for unhurried bathing or showering. The large mirror above the basins reflects natural light and increases the impression of spaciousness. Sliding cupboard door fronts have been designed to keep essential but mundane items concealed, and echo the Japanese theme underlying this calm, efficient layout.

SHARED BATHROOM CHOICE

△ OPPOSITE CORNERS
Placing the bath and the shower opposite one another ensures that conversations can continue when both are in use. Planned space for bathrobes and essentials has been designed for each user to keep their belongings within easy reach.

△ ANGLED LAYOUT
A corner bath and shower butted up against one another make full use of the space, allowing two people to use the room in comfort. Basins placed side by side with storage below keep the area clutter-free.

△ DOUBLE SHOWER
A large double shower unit rather than a single shower and bath may be more suited to your lifestyle. It can save on water consumption and speed up time spent in the bathroom. It can be shared with a partner or muddy children can be piled in to wash. Choose hardwearing ceramic tiles for the interior, especially if the shower is frequently used.

SPACE TO MOVE ▷
Although it is possible for two people to share a standard-sized bathroom, it may be cramped. Here a spare bedroom is converted into a luxuriously large shared bathroom. Space out the items of sanitaryware so that each piece is easy to access. Plan the space to allow for a large freestanding bath, shower, and a chair for towels and clothes.

UNUSUAL SHAPE BATHROOM PLAN

THE INCREASING demands of homeowners for ensuite bathrooms often means that in a house the largest bedroom is divided up or a bathroom is squeezed in under the eaves. Both of these solutions can leave you with an irregular-shaped room with little natural light. Imaginative planning, however, can ensure that the sanitaryware is well situated, and that irregular walls and odd angles are an asset, not a drawback.

ROOF SKYLIGHT
Light filters through a roof panel in each partition, making the bathroom brighter.

MOSAIC TILES
Lining the shower area, mosaic protects the walls from damp.

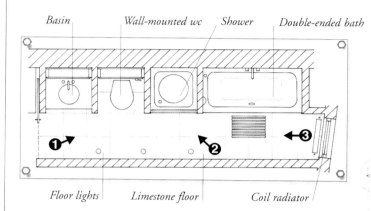

Basin   Wall-mounted wc   Shower   Double-ended bath

Floor lights   Limestone floor   Coil radiator

△ **BIRD'S EYE VIEW**
A long, narrow space under the gabled roof has been cleverly divided to create a galley-style bathroom. All the sanitaryware sits in a row along one wall for an uncomplicated plumbing run, while a corridor along the length of the room connects the different activity zones.

INTERNAL ROOM
DIMENSIONS:
1.6m (5ft 2in) wide
4.9m (15ft 9in) long

△ ❶ **ALL ON ONE SIDE**
Placing the basin, wc, shower, and bath along the left-hand side of the room while keeping the right-hand side of the bathroom free to walk between each item, is inspirational planning. Partitions create identities for each activity zone without the need for doors, so the room feels light and spacious.

SLIDING DOOR
A space-saving sliding door opens and closes without interrupting the basin area.

PARTITION
The wall offers privacy while allowing air to flow freely.

FLOOR LIGHTS
Sealed halogen units are safe for bathroom use as they are low voltage and water-resistant.

SHOWER INTERIOR ❷ ▷

The shower cubicle stands in the middle of the roof area – where the ceiling is highest – so that there is ample room for showering. The cubicle is subjected to a regular soaking so the walls are clad in mosaic tiles for a hardwearing, waterproof finish, which combined with quality door seals prevents water seepage.

ROLLER BLINDS
Blinds take up little space and allow diffused light to pass into the room.

SLOPING CEILING
A bath under the eaves makes good use of space; you sit up without hitting your head.

COIL RADIATOR
Occupying a small floor area, a coil heats the air as it rises.

FOR MORE DETAILS...

Shower and bath fittings
SEE PP.28–29

Wall-mounted wc SEE P.35

Limestone flooring SEE P.43

Mosaic wallcovering
SEE P.45

▽ ❸ DESIGN DETAIL

Stone flooring is water-resistant and is ideally suited to heavy-wear areas such as the narrow passage between each item of sanitaryware. Sealed floor lights sunk into the limestone tiles are shatterproof, and produce a soft diffused light that illuminates the length of the walkway and adds character.

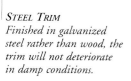

STEEL TRIM
Finished in galvanized steel rather than wood, the trim will not deteriorate in damp conditions.

DESIGN POINTS

■ Showers fit into most small and awkward areas but make sure they are well lit or they can be hazardous.

■ Good ventilation is essential – even more so when space is limited and air-flow restricted. Plan the position of the extractor fan opposite the door where it will draw fresh air in.

■ Keep colours and patterns simple in a small bathroom, and avoid fussy fittings.

UNUSUAL SHAPE BATHROOM CHOICE

△ CORNER SOLUTION
If you do not have the wall space to fit a standard bath, a corner bath may solve the problem. A shower rose and curtain rail suspended over the bath mean that it can double up as a shower cubicle; the curtain can be pulled to one side to let light in.

▽ MEZZANINE FLOOR
A good architect will pay dividends when faced with a studio conversion. Here, a high-ceilinged room is divided up to create a spectacular ensuite bathroom on the upper level. A tensile steel structure offers a strong platform for the fittings.

△ DEEP TUB
A deep bath tub makes the best use of space in a small room. A bath and shower mixer tap offers a sit-down shower option. Shelves and a towel rail make use of the wall space, and an offset basin leaves room for the door to open.

△ IRREGULAR LEVELS
The floor of this bathroom drops deeply into a small recess, making the perfect place to sink a bath. Once lying down in the bath, the windows are no threat to privacy. Clear glass roof panels allow light to flood into this small room.

SUNKEN BATH ▷
Recessing a bath into the floor is an imaginative way to create the illusion of space. The underside of the bath is cushioned for protection and the weight of the marble walls and tiles are taken by the solid floor. Glass blocks replace the window, filtering the light.

PLAN YOUR DESIGN

PLOT YOUR ROOM

THE STARTING POINT for designing any bathroom is the floor plan and elevations. The following steps will help you to measure up the room. Then, transfer the dimensions onto graph paper to give scale drawings that you can refer to when planning the layout.

EQUIPMENT
This basic equipment for drawing and measuring will help you to record the bathroom's dimensions, service points, and any irregular architectural features. These will determine where you place your items of sanitaryware, radiators, light fittings, and storage units.

NOTEPAD TAPE MEASURE

FLOOR DIMENSIONS

Before installing a bathroom, you must have an understanding of the plumbing layout. Check that pipework is in the right place for your choice of wc, bath, radiator, and basin, and, if not, budget for any plumbing alterations. Familiarize yourself with the shape of the room and the position of windows as these will also dictate the design. Consult the floor plan when choosing furniture to check that items fit into the available space.

❶ SKETCH THE ROOM
Begin by standing in the middle of the room, looking down at the floor. Draw a rough sketch with a soft pencil, starting at the door and working clockwise around the room. Include fixed architectural features.

❷ MEASURE THE FLOOR
Next, plot the dimensions of the room by measuring the total floor area. Place the tape measure across the room and note down the width on your sketch in a coloured pen. Ignore any details such as the skirting boards at this early stage.

❸ PLOT WALL LENGTH
Next work around the room, measuring each wall length in turn. Remember that not all walls are symmetrical or at right angles to one another, so take care to provide an accurate survey of their lengths.

❹ AWKWARD CORNERS
Recesses and projections need careful measuring to ensure that they are correct on the plan. If necessary, take a photograph to keep with the plans to provide a visual guide to irregular shapes, or make a paper template for future use.

❺ PLOT SERVICE POINTS
Plot the position of service points, such as water, waste, electrics, and the soil pipe on your plan. Make a note of their distance from any corners. To avoid long unsightly ducting, try to place the wc as close as possible to the soil pipe.

❻ CHECK DISTANCES
Note the distances between existing pipe runs for the central heating and water supply so that items will fit when placed side by side. If you need to move pipes, a plumber should be able to work out the cost from your plan.

WALL ELEVATIONS

Drawing and measuring the elevations is a valuable exercise as it will help you to decide whether a basin or wc can fit beneath a window, or if furniture will obstruct ventilation ducts or radiators. Elevations are useful if you are installing items like a high-level wc (*see p.34*) as a tall wall is needed for the cistern to flush.

❶ RECORD THE HEIGHT
Measure from the floor to the window sill as some basin and cistern designs are higher than average and may not fit the space. Noting the position of the window will also help you to plan extra lighting in dark corners.

❷ RECORD DISTANCES
Measure the blank wall space from the window to the nearest corner to check that curtains will not obstruct the window and reduce the light level. Also, measure the area from the top of the window to the ceiling.

DRAWING-UP SCALE PLANS

From your survey (created following the steps on the facing page) you have the information you need to work out approximately where to position furniture and sanitaryware in the room. If you wish to create a more detailed drawing, plot the floor plan and wall elevations to scale on graph paper, using the advice below.

SERVICE POINTS
Crosses show the water supply and circles the waste outlets.

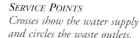

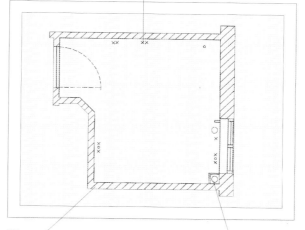

WALLS
Use a narrow border of cross-hatching for internal walls and a thicker border for external.

❷ DRAW UP AN ELEVATION ▷
Referring to the measurements on your rough sketch elevations, draw up each wall to scale. Mark on the window catches and door handles and indicate which way they open. Draw in any service pipes to help you decide what alterations may be required for you to achieve your ideal bathroom layout.

❸ OTHER ELEVATIONS ▽
Reserve space on your external wall elevation for a ventilation system, and plan the rest so the room's features are unobstructed.

YOU WILL NEED
Metric and imperial graph paper is supplied with this book, but you will also need a set square, ruler, pen, pencil, pencil sharpener, and rubber.

◁❶ TRANSFER THE FLOOR PLAN
Taking the precise measurements from your rough sketch, draw the four perimeter walls to scale on graph paper. Use a set square to join corners and straight lines. Next, plot the existing features that are important for planning, such as the soil stack, water supply, door opening, and windows.

SOIL STACK
All the waste will drain from this pipe.

CORNICE DEPTH
A deep cornice will interrupt a tall cistern or cupboard.

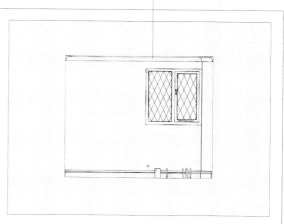

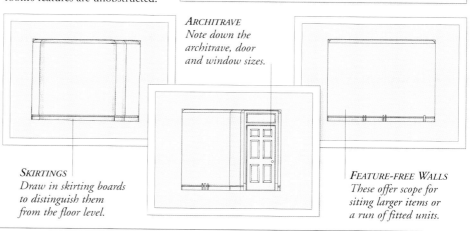

ARCHITRAVE
Note down the architrave, door and window sizes.

SKIRTINGS
Draw in skirting boards to distinguish them from the floor level.

FEATURE-FREE WALLS
These offer scope for siting larger items or a run of fitted units.

PLACE THE FEATURES

HAVING COMPILED A LIST of your preferred sanitaryware, furniture, and fittings, and mapped out your room plan on graph paper, you should have all the information at your fingertips to be able to work out the best arrangement of features in the bathroom. Try out several different design layouts by placing tracing paper over the scaled-down plan (*see pp.78–79*) and drawing on the elements. You may have to work up several versions, and analyze the pros and cons of each, before reaching a satisfactory solution.

TRACING PAPER

MASKING TAPE

SET SQUARE

PEN
SHARPENER
PENCIL
RUBBER

RULER

EQUIPMENT ▷
Take the room plan that you have drawn to scale and, using masking tape, stick a sheet of tracing paper over the top. With a soft pencil, draw the features; the ruler and set square will give accurate lines. Plan each new design on a fresh sheet of tracing paper.

DESIGN GUIDELINES

In order to achieve a successful finished plan, the elements for the bathroom need to be considered together. When designing your space, bear the following points in mind:

❶ Do not estimate the size of your selected items. Manufacturers' brochures include the exact dimensions of sanitaryware. Use these to draw each piece to scale on your plan.

❷ By keeping bathroom pipe runs simple you will limit the level of disruption and the cost of plumbing. Whenever possible, place items of sanitaryware along adjacent walls so that supply pipes and waste pipes run tidily and efficiently under the floorboards.

❸ The position of the wc is dictated by the fact that it needs to be close to the soil stack which expels waste into the mains sewage. The soil pipe from the wc must have sufficient "drop" from the stack in order to discharge solid waste. Soil pipes are also wider than waste water pipes and look best hidden behind ducting to be less obtrusive.

REJECTED PLANS

Arriving at a well-planned, ergonomic design takes time. Look at the position of each item on the plan and imagine what it would be like, in practice, to use the facilities where you have placed them. Remember that space is needed around each item for ease of use, and sanitaryware near the door must not restrict access.

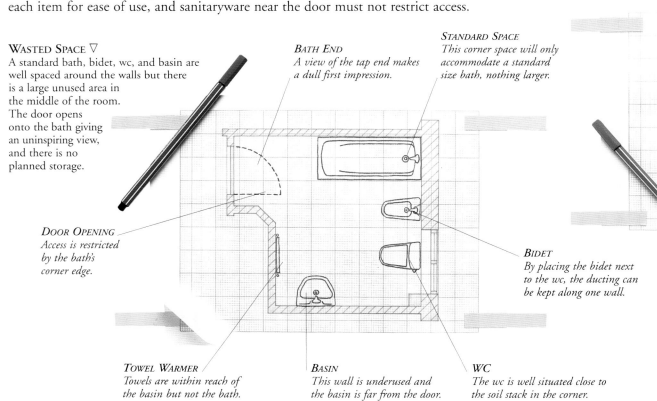

DOOR SWING
The door will open onto the person using the basin closest to the door.

WASTED SPACE ▽
A standard bath, bidet, wc, and basin are well spaced around the walls but there is a large unused area in the middle of the room. The door opens onto the bath giving an uninspiring view, and there is no planned storage.

BATH END
A view of the tap end makes a dull first impression.

STANDARD SPACE
This corner space will only accommodate a standard size bath, nothing larger.

DOOR OPENING
Access is restricted by the bath's corner edge.

BIDET
By placing the bidet next to the wc, the ducting can be kept along one wall.

BIDET
Wall sp... either s... is waste...

TOWEL WARMER
Towels are within reach of the basin but not the bath.

BASIN
This wall is underused and the basin is far from the door.

WC
The wc is well situated close to the soil stack in the corner.

SUCCESSFUL PLAN

Having assessed the advantages and disadvantages of each bathroom plan, and worked out the most ergonomic configuration of sanitaryware and other fittings, plot the most successful design onto graph paper in ink pen. You are now ready to consider design details, such as your wallcovering, flooring, and lighting needs.

DOOR SWING
Access is unrestricted and offers a good view of all the bathroom's facilities.

STORAGE
Towels and toiletries are kept on open shelving with cleaning products stored behind lockable doors at the base.

PERFECT SOLUTION ▷
The curved shower echoes the shape of the corner bath opposite, while a built-in unit stores essentials tidily, creating a bathroom that looks luxurious and is a pleasure to use. Two radiators, one by the door and one next to the shower, keep the room warm.

SINGLE BASIN
The basin is unobstructed by a radiator or bath.

CORNER BATH
Space around the bath makes it easy to climb in and out.

BIDET
Placed next to the wc, the bidet is easy to use and plumbing is simple.

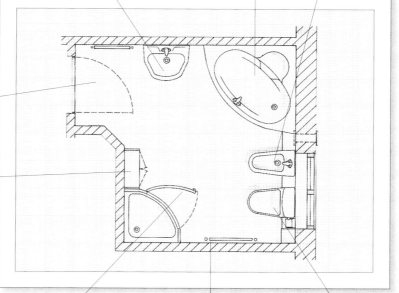

SHOWER DOOR
The curved shower door opens into the room.

TOWEL RADIATOR
Warm towels are within reach of the shower.

WC
There is room to sit in comfort on the wc.

LACK OF SPACE
Space around the basins is very limited. There is insufficient elbow room for two people to use the area at the same time.

ISOLATED WC
Poor planning leaves a lot of space around the wc while other elements are too crowded.

RADIATOR
A corner position restricts warm air circulation.

△ NO STORAGE PROVISION
By changing the orientation of the bath and adding a second basin, the wall space to the left of the door is better used but cramped. The bath doubles up as a shower, and while the bidet and wc are well spaced, storage cupboards for towels, lavatory rolls, and toiletries have been overlooked.

CROWDED SANITARYWARE ▽
Replacing the standard bath with a corner bath has made better use of wall space but the door area is still crowded. By re-locating the other items of sanitaryware, there is now room for a shower.

INTERRUPTED USE
The basin is much too close to the bidet and bathroom door for it to be functional.

CRAMPED POSITION
Lack of leg room either side of the bidet makes it uncomfortable to use.

CORNER BATH
The corner bath frees up more bathroom wall space by cutting into the area in the centre of the room.

DOOR OPENING
The basin is too close to the door, restricting access.

SHOWER
The corner of the shower juts out into the room and there is no towel rail nearby.

WC
Close to the soil stack, the wc leaves room next to the bath for a radiator.

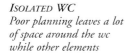

PLANNING DETAIL

NOW THAT THE BATHROOM LAYOUT has been resolved, you can start choosing details, such as sanitaryware colours, cupboard finishes, wallcoverings, flooring, lighting, and fittings that match your bathroom needs. Apart from the initial purchase price of items, take into account the total cost of the plumbing and installation, and how long the work will take, and plan accordingly.

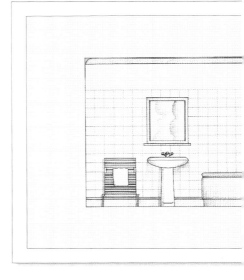

◁ COLLECT PICTURES
Interiors and home-interest magazines can provide you with inspiration. Cut out fittings and bathrooms that interest you and note down the addresses and telephone numbers of stockists.

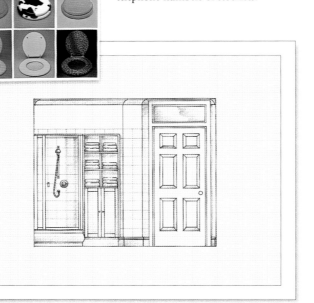

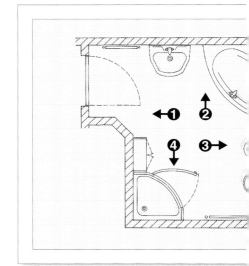

△ ❶ SHOWER AND STORAGE AREA
Draw in the sanitaryware and fittings to help you visualize how they will fit into the space you have allocated. Here, the storage unit has been built to the same height as the shower so the top of the wall is free and the room appears taller. The storage unit has been divided up into open shelving and cupboards to help organize products.

◁ PRODUCT BROCHURES
Collect manfacturers' brochures so that you have full details of their range of products. Specialist bathroom showrooms should also be able to provide product information. Keep this literature to hand when planning the room as it contains the dimensions, range of styles, colour choices, and price lists.

❹ LADDER RAIL ▷
A tall ladder radiator next to the shower enclosure shows how well this wall elevation has been planned. The radiator warms this end of the room and heats up towels that are easy to reach when you step out of the shower. A robe hook is another useful detail.

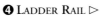

MATERIAL SAMPLES ▷
Collect samples showing sanitaryware colours, flooring materials, and wallcoverings. Keep a collection of your favourite items to help you make your style decisions.

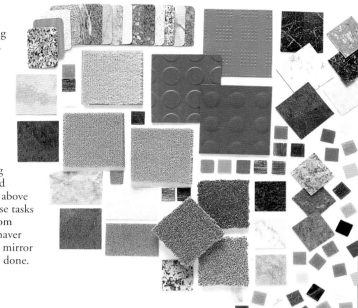

◁ ❷ BASIN ELEVATION
The bath and towel radiator leaves "elbow room" around the basin area for performing activities, such as shaving and applying make-up. A mirror above the basin area helps with these tasks and reflects light into the room from the window. Install a shaver socket close to the basin and mirror when other electrical work is done.

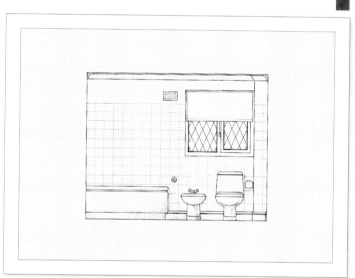

▷ FLOOR PLAN
Number the walls on your floor plan and copy the same numbers onto the corresponding elevation so that you can see at-a-glance exactly where each element is placed within the room.

△ ❸ WALL DETAIL
Plot the bath, bidet, and wc elevation to check that there is plenty of leg room on either side of the sanitaryware, and that there is space behind for ducting to hide the wide soil pipe. Details such as a lavatory roll holder and towel hook are also planned at a suitable height, as is an unobtrusive extractor grille for this outside wall.

COLOUR SCHEMES ▷
Although colour choice is a matter of personal taste, bear in mind that pale shades will make a bathroom appear more spacious while dark tones absorb light and make it look smaller. Remember that different surface finishes affect the quality of light. High gloss paint finishes and shiny tiles increase reflections and glare while matt finishes diffuse light.

WHAT NEXT?

■ When you have a clear idea of what you want, take your finished design to a bathroom showroom, plumber, or design company to help put all your ideas into action. If structural work is required you may need to contact an architect. He or she will be able to advise you on planning regulations or health and safety restrictions.

■ It is important to plan the order of work in advance as a cast of builders, plumbers, electricians, fitters, tilers, and decorators may be involved. The work should proceed as follows: structural changes, electrical wiring, plumbing and fitting of sanitaryware and cupboards, wall tiling, flooring, and lastly decoration. The exception to this is if you want fitted carpets, which should be installed last.

■ Delivery times for fittings and sanitaryware can be long, so check that the goods you have ordered will be delivered in your time frame. When they arrive, make sure that they are as ordered, and undamaged.

BUDGET TIPS

■ It is easy to go over budget when choosing both your sanitaryware and fittings, and difficult to find inexpensive alternatives of similar quality. For this reason, inquire about ex-display bathrooms from plumbers' merchants and showrooms, which can offer excellent value for money.

■ A bathroom tiled from floor to ceiling can be prohibitively expensive but, if this is your preferred finish, opt for pure white or plain coloured tiles, which are cheaper than patterned tiles. To prevent the bathroom from looking too clinical, use the more expensive patterned or profile tiles in a border to add interest.

STOCKISTS AND SUPPLIERS

The following directory of useful names and addresses will help you source the shops needed to furnish and equip your bathroom. The letters (*MO*) after an entry indicate that items are available by mail order; some retailers may operate a mail order service as well as selling through a shop (*Also available MO*). If you are considering structural work, it is advisable to consult your builder or an architect.

BATHROOM SPECIALISTS

ALTERNATIVE PLANS
9 Hester Road
London SW11 4AN
Tel: 0171 228 6460
Contemporary and traditional sanitaryware and fittings with planning and installation service.

ARMITAGE SHANKS BATHROOMS
Armitage
Rugeley
Staffordshire WS15 4BT
Tel: 01543 490253
Manufacturers of a wide range of sanitaryware and showers.

ASTON MATHEWS LTD
141-147a Essex Road
London N1 2SN
Tel: 0171 226 7220
Bathroom specialists with a wide range of sanitaryware, fittings, and accessories. (Also available MO).

BEGGS & PARTNERS
Great Patrick Street
Belfast
Northern Ireland
BT1 2NX
Tel: 01232 235791
Stockists of major manufacturers' sanitaryware offering planning and installation.

BUBBLE LUXURY BATHROOMS
11-13 Chalmers Street
Dunfermline
KY12 8AT
Tel: 01383 624777
Specialists in spa baths, whirlpools, saunas, and steam rooms with installation service. (Also available MO).

CP HART
Newnham Terrace
Hercules Road
London SE1 7DR
Tel: 0171 902 1000
Supply and installation of top-of-the-range bathroom fittings and furniture. (Also available MO).

DRUMMONDS OF BRAMLEY
Architectural Antiques Ltd
Birtley Farm
Horsham Road
Guildford GU5 OLA
Tel: 01483 898766
Specialist architectural salvage company offering renovated original fittings and sanitaryware; also a vitreous re-enamelling service for period baths.

GRAHAMS
29-35 Donaghadee Road
Newtownards
Northern Ireland BT23 8EH
Tel: 01247 813494
Stockists of sanitaryware produced by major manufacturers, bathroom furniture, tiles, and plumbing goods. Branches throughout the UK.

HERITAGE BATHROOMS PLC
Unit 1a, Princess Street
Beominster
Bristol BS3 4AG
Tel: 0117 963 9762
Traditional sanitaryware manufacturers with natural wood vanity units, panelling, and wc seats.

IDEAL-STANDARD LTD
The Bathroom Works
National Avenue
Kingston-upon-Hull
N. Yorks HU5 4HS
Tel: 01482 346461
Part of Europe's largest bathroom manufacturing group, producing high quality sanitaryware.

INVA-DEX LTD
66-68 Manchester Road
Chapel-en-le-Frith
Derbyshire SK12 6RZ
Tel: 01298 816366
Specialist bathroom fitting and sanitaryware for the less able. (Also available MO).

JACUZZI UK LTD
17 Mount Street
London W1Y 5RA
Tel: 0171 409 1776
Whirlpools, showers, and steam bathroom products and installation. (Also available MO).

JEWSON
58 Craigentinny Avenue
Edinburgh EH6 7LJ
Tel: 0131 554 1144
Stockists of sanitaryware produced by major manufacturers. Also bathroom furniture, tiles, and plumbing goods are available nationwide.

LEFROY BROOKS (LONDON) LTD
Unit 3, Marston Industrial Estate
Marston Road
Wolverhampton WV2 4LX
Tel: 01902 421922
Manufacturers of top quality traditional sanitaryware, fittings, and accessories.

MISCELLANEA OF CHURT
Crossways
Churt
Farnham
Surrey GU10 2JA
Tel: 01428 714014
Stockists of sanitaryware, fittings, and accessories; discontinued colours a speciality. (Also available MO).

NORDIC BATHROOMS
Dept DKG
Holland Road
Oxted
Surrey RH8 9BZ
Tel: 01883 732400
Glass bathroom furniture, shower, steam room, and sauna specialists. (Also available MO).

ORIGINAL BATHROOMS
143-145 Kew Road
Richmond
Surrey TW9 2PN
Tel: 0181 940 7554
Bathroom specialists providing a planning and installation service. (Also available MO).

RIPPLES
Chelsea House
London Road
Bath BA1 6DB
Tel: 01225 447971
Sanitaryware and fittings offering extensive range of products.

SITTING PRETTY BATHROOMS
122 Dawes Road
London SW6 7EG
Tel: 0171 381 0049
Suppliers of period-style sanitaryware.

THE WATER MONOPOLY

16-18 Lonsdale Road
London NW6 6RD
Tel: 0171 624 2636
Suppliers of restored antique English and French sanitaryware and fittings.

WEST ONE BATHROOMS LTD

60 Queenstown Road
London SW8 3RY
Tel: 0171 720 9333
Bathroom specialists providing a planning and installation service. Will source any product and custom build. (Also available MO).

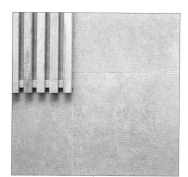

BATHROOM FITTINGS

ALLGOOD PLC

63-83 Brierley Street
Birmingham B19 3NT
Tel: 0121 359 4415
High quality stainless steel sanitaryware fittings. (Also available MO).

HANSGROHE LTD

Units D1 & D2
Sandown Park Trading Estate
Esher
Surrey KT10 8BL
Tel: 01372 465655
Innovative, top quality shower, bath, basin and bidet fittings.

HEWI (UK) LTD

Scimitar Close
Gillingham Business Park
Gillingham
Kent ME8 0RN
Tel: 01634 377688
Suppliers of brightly coloured nylon bathroom fittings. (Also available MO).

NEWMAN TONKS ARCHITECTURAL HARDWARE LTD

The Crescent
Birmingham Business Park
Birmingham B37 7YX
Tel: 0121 717 7777
Suppliers of coloured plastic bathroom fittings.

SAMUEL HEATH & SONS PLC

Cobden Works
Leopold Street
Birmingham B12 0UJ
Tel: 0121 772 2303
Wide selection of traditional taps and bathroom accessories with choice of finishes.

SHOWERS

AQUALISA PRODUCTS LTD

Flyers Way
Westerham
Kent TN16 1DE
Tel: 01959 560000
Suppliers of a wide choice of shower mixer valves, and a range of both power and electric showers.

MATKI PLC

Churchward Road
Yate
Bristol BS17 5PL
Tel: 01454 322888
Shower surrounds and shower trays.

SHOWERLUX (UK) LTD

Sibtree Road
Coventry
West Midlands CV3 4EL
Tel: 01203 639400
Shower trays, enclosures and custom-made shower rooms with designs for the less able.

TREVI SHOWERS

The Bathroom Works
National Avenue
Kingston-upon-Hull HU5 4HS
Tel: 01482 470788
Full range of shower controls and fittings.

WALLCOVERINGS, SURFACES, AND FLOORINGS

AMTICO

The Amtico Showroom
18 Hanover Square
London W1R 9BD
Tel: 0171 629 6258
Wide choice of flooring styles.

FORBO-NAIRN LTD

P.O. Box 1
Kircaldy
Fife KY1 2SB
Tel: 01592 643777
Manufacturers of sheet vinyl and natural mineral resin Marmoleum brand.

H&R JOHNSON TILES LTD

Highgate Tile Works
High Street
Tunstall
Stoke-on-Trent
Staffordshire ST6 4JX
Tel: 01782 575575
Extensive Prismatics range of colourful plain tiles.

DUPONT CORIAN®

Tel: 0800 962116
Custom-made mineral resin surfaces for countertops, walls, and showers.

HEATING AND VENTILATION

BISQUE

15 Kingsmead Square
Bath
BA1 2AE
Tel: 01225 469244
Colourful and contemporary heated towel rails and radiators. (Also available MO).

DIMPLEX

Manor House Avenue
Millbrook
Southampton SO15 0AW
Tel: 01703 777117
Heated towel rails and wall-mounted bathroom fans.

JAGA HEATING PRODUCTS

Jaga House
Orchard Business Park
Bromyard Road
Ledbury HR8 1LG
Tel: 01531 631533
Heated bath panels and mirror radiators.

MYSON

Victoria Works
Nelson Street
Bolton
Lancashire BL3 2DW
Tel: 01204 382017
Towel warmers and recessed plinth heaters.

XPELAIR LTD

P.O. Box 220
Deykin Avenue
Witton
Birmingham B6 7JH
Tel: 0121 327 1984
Air extractors, vents, and heat recovery units. (Also available MO).

INDEX

ACKNOWLEDGMENTS

AUTHOR'S ACKNOWLEDGMENTS

There are many people to thank for their hard work and assistance in producing this book: All those who allowed us into their homes to photograph their bathrooms; the team at Dorling Kindersley whose interest and enthusiasm made the book a pleasure to write. Thanks firstly to Mary-Clare Jerram and Charlotte Davies for offering the marvellous opportunity to write *Bathroom*. To the Editor, Bella Pringle who deserves much credit for her skill, dedication, and encouragement. Thanks too, to Sharon Moore and Clive Hayball who worked tirelessly on the design and layout. Thanks also to Richard Lee whose beautiful illustrations and room plans have brought life to the practical drawings.

Thanks to Isobel Coomber, John Laughton, and Robin Levien from the Ideal-Standard team and Leftley Bros Ltd for their support and help. To my mother for entertaining the children when away on location and meetings – no mean feat.

Finally, a special thank you must go to my husband Nelson who has juggled his career, the children, and menagerie to provide me with uninterrupted hours of writing; and still found time to read drafts and offer ideas.

PUBLISHER'S ACKNOWLEDGMENTS

Dorling Kindersley would like to thank: Ally Ireson for picture research, Hilary Bird for the index, Shani Zion for additional styling, and Andrew Nash for design assistance. We would like to thank the architects whose plans appear in the book: Plan pp.48-49 Ken Rorrison, Bushcow Henley, 27-29 Whitfield Street, London, W1P 5RB, 0171 379 6391; Plan pp.68-69 Dale Loth Architects, 1 Cliff Road, London, NW1 9AJ, 0171 485 4003; Plan pp.72-73 Joyce Owens, Azman Owens Architect, 109 Clifton Street, London, EC2 4LD, 0171 739 8404.

We are indebted to the following individuals who generously allowed us to photograph in their homes: Richard Blair-Oliphant; Sheila Fitzjones; Samantha Harrison; Richard and Pauline Lay; John Pemberton; Sharon Reed and William Sargent.

We would like to thank the following companies for allowing us to photograph in their showrooms and showhomes: Alternative Plans 31bl, 31tr, 33tr, 33br, 33bc, 33bl, 35tl, 36 bl, 36cr; C.P. Hart 12b, 22c, 26c, 29tl, 30bl, 31tl, 32t, 32b, 32cr, 34bl, 37br, 38tr, 38br, 43tl, 44br, 45tc, 45bl, 45br; Leftley Bros Ltd 78-79; Original Bathrooms 10t, 23br, 29bl, 35cr, 37tl, 37bl, 42tr; Sitting Pretty 30t, 32cl, 34r, 35bcr; The Water Monopoly 9t, 16t, 25br, 25cr, 29c, 87br, 88; West One 24cl, 24cr, 25tr, 26bl, 27tl, 27 tr, 28bl, 28cr, 28tr, 29tr, 29cr, 29cl, 29bc, 31br, 33t, 33cl, 33cr, 35cl, 35bcl, 35tr, 41bc.

We would also like to thank the following individuals and companies who lent us items for photography: Alternative Plans; Aston Matthews; Bisque Radiators 38bl; Bobo 35br; Christy Towels; Cologne & Cotton; Descamps; Fiona Craig-McFeely; Habitat; The Holding Company; Innovations; Muji; Natural Products; Newman Tonks Architectural Hardware; Smith & Nephew; The Pier; Pru Bury; Mr Tomkinson Carpets; The Source; Yves Delorme, Ever Trading.

ARTWORK

Room artworks by Richard Lee.
Ergonomic diagrams by David Ashby.

PHOTOGRAPHY

All photographs by Jake Fitzjones except:
Andy Crawford 17r, 19t, 29br, 35br, 37tr, 38bl, 39tr, 39c, 43bl, 43br, 45tl, 76-77, 80-81, 82-83, 86br.
Earl Carter/Belle/Arcaid (Designer: Christian Liagre) 50bl; David Churchill/Arcaid (Architect: Elspeth Beard) 74b; Mike Crockett/Elizabeth Whiting & Associates (Designer: Fiona Cowan) 75; Michael Dunne/Elizabeth Whiting & Associates 66b; Andreas von Einsiedel/National Trust Picture Library 6tl, Andreas von Einsiedel/ Elizabeth Whiting & Associates 74tr; Aki Furudate (Architect: Bramante Architects) 40br; Chris Gascoigne/View (Architect: Simon Conder) 25cl; Dennis Gilbert/View (Architect: Rick Mather) 40tl, (Architect: Bernhard Blauel) 51, (Architect: AHMM) 70cr; Rodney Hyett/ Elizabeth Whiting & Associates 45bc, 74tl; IMS/Camera Press 54tr, 66tr; Simon Kenny/ Belle/Arcaid (Designer: Andrew Nimmo & Annabel Lahz) 74cr; Suomen Kuvapalvelu/ Camera Press 44cl; John Edward Linden/Arcaid (Architect: John Newton) 14-15, (Architect: Julian Powell Tuck) 54tl; Living/Camera Press 58tl; Nadia Mackenzie (Designer Francois Gilles/IPL Interiors) 50tl, (Owner: Paula Pryke) 55, (The Water Monopoly) 66tl; Marianne Majerus (Architect: Barbara Weiss) 70t; Simon McBride (Designer: Kaffe Fasset) 42tl, (Owner: Merete Steinboch) 70-71; James Mortimer/National Trust Picture Library 6-7; Ian Parry/ Abode 58tr, 59; David Parmiter 58br; Spike Powell/ Elizabeth Whiting & Associates 54bl; Jo Reid and John Peck (Architect: Simon Conder) 27bl; Elizabeth Whiting & Associates 70bl; SchonerWohnen/ Camera Press 62tl, 66-67; Friedholm Thomas/Elizabeth Whiting & Associates 62bl; Petrina Tinslay/Arcaid (Designer: Phil & Jackie Staub) 63; Henry Wilson/Interior Archive (Designer: Patrick Jefferson) 58bl.

The following companies kindly lent us photographs: Antique Baths of Ivybridge 25tl; Jacuzzi UK 24bl; Armitage Shanks 8tc; Ideal-Standard 22tr; Dimplex 39tc; Jaga 39tl; Shires 23tr; Lefroy Brooks 23bl; Mira 29tc; Myson 39cl; Novatec 41tl; Showerlux 22cr, 27bl; Twyfords 35bl; Vent-Axia 39bl, bc.

Every effort has been made to trace the copyright holders. We apologize for any omission and would be pleased to insert these in subsequent editions.

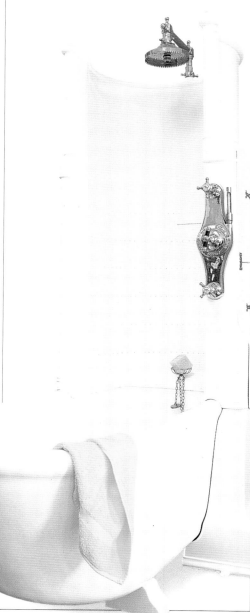

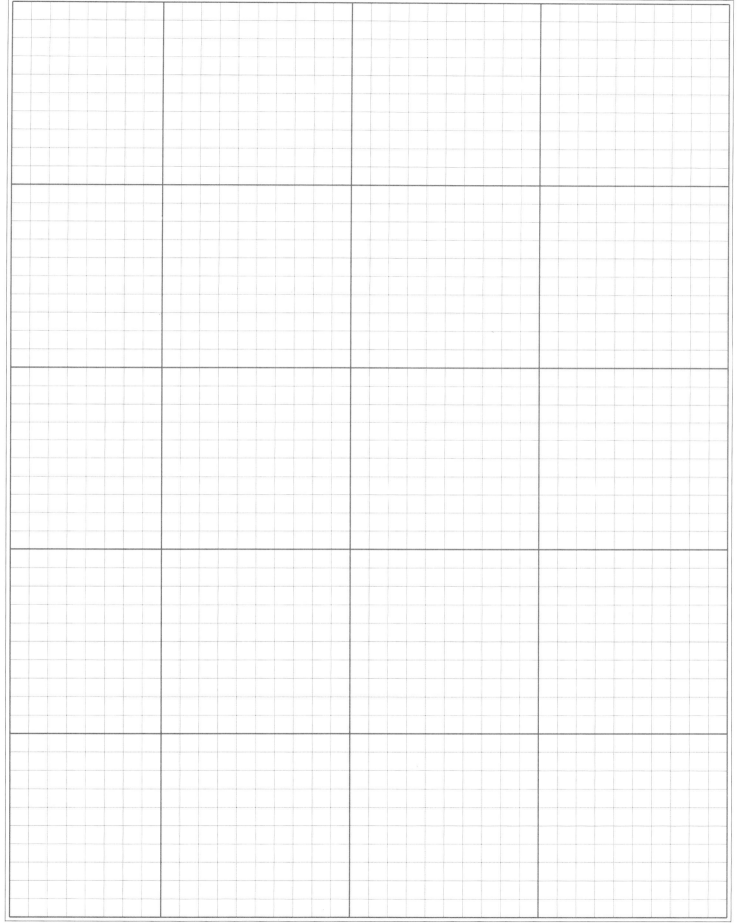

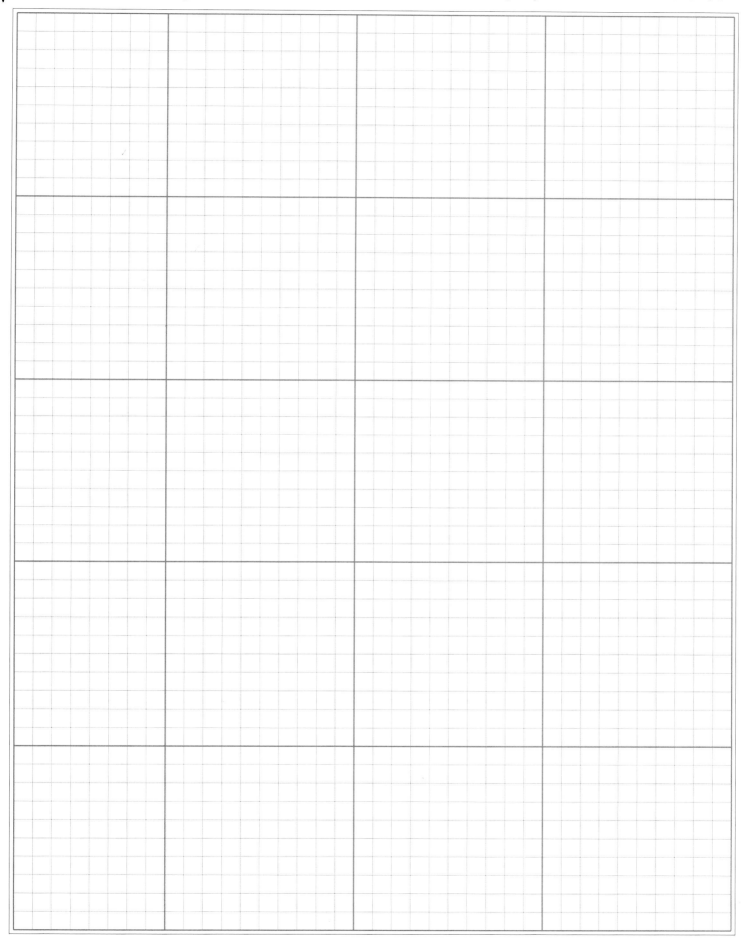

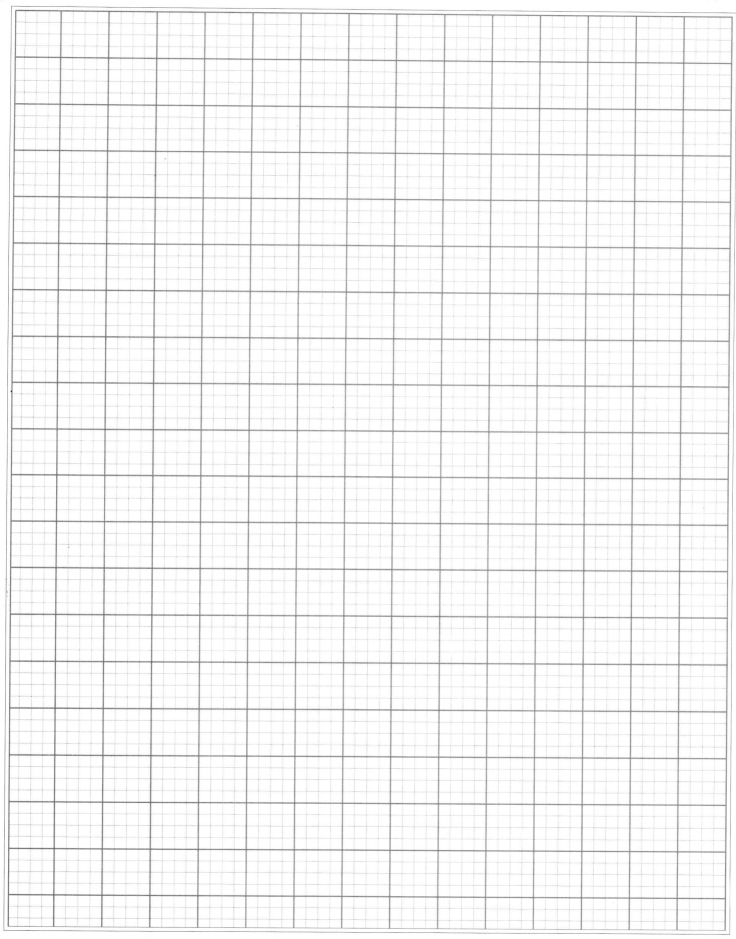